Design and Launch an Online

Boutique

in a WEEK

Other Titles in the Click Start Series

Design and Launch an E-Commerce Business in a Week

Design and Launch an Online Gift Business in a Week

Design and Launch an Online Travel Business in a Week

Design and Launch an Online Networking Business in a Week

Entrepreneur MAGAZINE'S
CLICKSTARTS

Design and Launch an Online

Boutique

in a WEEK

- ◆ Complete Guide to Creating a Specialized Store
- ◆ In-the-Trenches Advice from Successful E-Tailers
- ◆ For Even the Most Technically Challenged

Entrepreneur Press & Melissa Campanelli

EP
Entrepreneur.
Press

5050301081 2800

Jere L. Calmes, Publisher
Cover Design: Desktop Miracles
Production and Composition: Eliot House Productions

Computer icon ©Skocko
Hand icon ©newyear2008

Library of Congress Cataloging-in-Publication Data
Campanelli, Melissa.
   Design and launch an online boutique in a week/by Entrepreneur Press and Melissa Campanelli.
      p.   cm.   —(Click start series)
   ISBN-13: 978-1-59918-188-2 (alk. paper)
   ISBN-10: 1-59918-188-6
      1. Electronic commerce. 2. Retail trade. 3. New business enterprises. I. Entrepreneur Press. II. Title.
   HF5548.32.C3553 2008
   658.8'72—dc22   2008015786

Printed in Canada

13 12 11 10 09 08   10 9 8 7 6 5 4 3 2 1

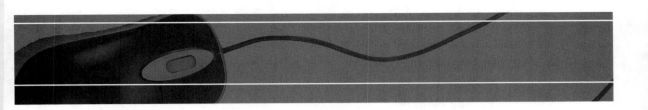

Contents

Chapter 6

E-Commerce Turnkey Solutions _ 67

Chapter 7

Inventory and Fulfillment _ 93

Acknowledgments

*T*his book could not have been written without Entrepreneur Press' Jere Calmes and Courtney Thurman, who not only served as my supervisors, but also encouraged and challenged me throughout the process of writing of this book. Eliot House Production's Karen Billipp was also indispensible. Together, these folks all patiently guided me through this project, never accepting less than my best efforts. I thank them all.

I also thank all the wonderful online boutique owners who I interviewed for this book, they all had interesting, enlightening stories to share and offered inspiration.

Finally, I thank my family, who has provided support, encouragement, and laughter. The book is dedicated to my husband, Rob, to whom I owe so much.

—Melissa Campanelli
Brooklyn, New York, 2008

Online Retail: Art or Science?

Bluefly CMO, Bradford Matson, Hypothesizes

*C*lick Start: Design and Launch an Online Boutique in a Week* is the perfect introduction to the ever-changing world of online retail—where you can sell anything—and track everything. Not so at a bricks-and-mortar store or even in a catalog business. Being online means being on the hook for every single move your customer makes. You determine exactly what the customer sees, you architect exactly how the customer interacts with your product and you get immediate feedback. How great is that: you're in total control with all the information you could ever ask for. Until, of course, you're not.

So, if you're set on launching a luxury e-business in a week here's the best piece of advice I can share with you. A smart colleague and direct marketing guru once told me that the key to understanding this business is to start at the end of the process and work back to the beginning, keeping a record of relevant data points along the way. You'll find its easy enough to pour visitors into the top of your funnel. Real success is measured in conversion. The better you are at closing the sale the more scalable your business. Starting at the end keeps the focus on what your customer really wants from you: your product. Then you can move on to optimizing the experience and for us marketers, analyzing and interpreting the behavioral data is the only way we can truly deliver a positive and satisfying shopping experience. This is no guessing game, folks. This is science. It's what you do with that science that turns it into art.

And how do you make art out of numbers and behavior patterns? Give your customers the product they want the way they want it. Use the data they give you with every click to create a meaningful relationship with them. Customers who love what they buy and how they buy it are the best retention AND acquisition plan.

As CMO of Bluefly.com, people often ask me if keeping up with the constant changes in the economy, customer behavior, and new product coming in every day is relentless. My answer is always the same: YES. But it's incredibly exhilarating too. Before I joined Bluefly I spent many years in the catalog business, which now seems like eons ago both in time elapsed and in relevance. It's intensely rewarding to be part of where consumer culture is going. Sure, we may be making it up as we go along, but it's a wild ride and I'm loving every minute of it.

—Bradford Matson, CMO Bluefly.com

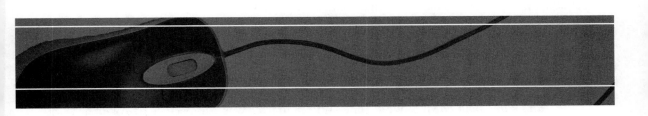

Preface

$\mathcal{I}$n mid-2007, after I completed my first book, *Open an Online Business in 10 Days*, I helped the folks at Entrepreneur Press start up a new series called "Click Starts." The focus of the series? To help fledgling netrepreneurs start specific types of e-businesses inexpensively and in less than a week.

After completing the *Online* book, it became clear to me that—thanks to a barrage of new technology developments—it is easier than ever for people to open an online business quickly and success-fully.

One of the book ideas we came up with was *Click Start: Design and Launch an Online Boutique in a Week.* The subject matter was the perfect fit for me: A woman who has lived in the New York area her whole life—a part of the country where fashion and boutiques are part of the fabric of everyday living. So, here and for the next 200 or so pages, please enjoy the fruits of my labor.

What I learned from researching and writing this book is that it is just as easy to open an online boutique as it is to open a traditional online shop. Why? Because not only are there easy-to-use and inexpensive website building tools, there are rich media and photography tools—which are key for online boutiquers. In addition, it is easier than ever to market online boutiques, thanks to a bevy of new social media tools, shopping bots, and other online marketing tactics.

However, keep in mind: For every online boutique that flourishes, hundreds—maybe thousands—go bust. What does it take to build an online boutique that will grow and succeed? Read this book and you'll know, because in these pages you'll find recipes for success and interviews with online boutique owners who know how to make it work online.

Websites—and online boutiques—are still being launched everyday—and making it to the big time—but now more than ever, they require a unique combination of customer insight, business understanding, technical know-how, financial resources, and entrepreneurial drive. The possibilities of success remain enticing, even when wallets are thin—if your ideas are smart and your execution persistent.

The goal of this book is to give you the tools and knowledge you'll need to emerge among the victors. In these pages, you'll learn everything there is to know about starting—and running—your online boutique. You'll find the soup to nuts, the A to Z, of taking your idea through funding, launching, winning eyeballs, and laughing all the way to the bank.

You'll find out what you need and where to get it. The first few chapters will cover everything to do to get your online boutique up and running—and this can really be done in a week. These chapters include the basics, such as writing a business plan, figuring out your niche market, setting prices, buying the tools you need to get started, and setting up your website. The rest of the book will offer tools and tips related to how you can maintain your business, market, and even watch it grow.

Throughout all of these chapters, the book also features interviews, with successful online boutique owners, you'll also find sidebars and tip boxes scattered throughout the book, designed to hammer home key points.

Here's the promise of this book: if you want to find out everything you know about opening an online boutique, you'll find it between these covers. Read on to find out how to make your internet dreams a reality.

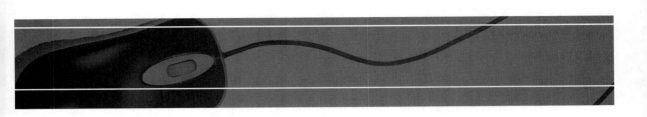

Introduction

*I*f you've picked up this book, you probably already know the internet offers a virtual universe of opportunity. Simply put, the internet is for real. In the 21st century if you're not on it, you're not in business. That is today's reality byte.

This book is specifically about selling high-end or luxury items in an online boutique. If you've picked it up, you are probably also aware that luxury items are big business because they are generally purchased by a desirable and growing target market—the affluent online consumer.

In fact, according to internet research firm eMarketer Inc. (emarketer.com), the number of affluent internet users in the United States is expected to grow to 57.1 million in 2011, from 43.7 million in 2006. That will be 27 percent of the online population in 2011, up from 24 percent in 2006.

What's more, when the affluent masses go online, they gravitate toward activities like shopping for luxury items such as jewelry. In addition to being big spenders, affluent online shoppers exhibit other characteristics that make them particularly desirable. They are frequent shoppers who buy from a variety of retailers, they often purchase gifts, they are influential within their communities, and best of all, they are critical to margin-focused managers because they are generally price insensitive. And shop they do. U.S. luxury e-commerce sales are expected to grow to $7 billion in 2010 from $2.5 billion in 2007, according to Forrester Research Inc. (forrester.com).

Why are luxury goods so popular? "There are enough seasoned online buyers who have had good experiences purchasing basic items such as books and DVDs online," says Jeffrey Grau, senior analyst at eMarketer, "so they have the confidence to take it to the next level and [make] a more complex, more sophisticated, expensive purchase."

Because you already have an awesome luxury product to sell online, this book will help you get your online boutique started quickly and easily, and with the lowest initial investment possible. Best of all, no previous business experience is necessary, and you don't need to know anything about computer programming thanks to the many e-commerce turnkey solutions currently available to online merchants.

It's important to understand that *Design and Launch an Online Boutique in a Week* is not about get-rich-quick schemes. What this book focuses on is how to sell luxury products online in the most profitable and efficient way possible; and how to do it in a week's time. It will also help you properly identify your target audience and then efficiently and cost-effectively reach them with appropriate marketing, advertising, and public relations.

This book will help you get started quickly, but it also does not guarantee that you'll start generating a profit overnight, or even within a few weeks. As you'll soon discover, once your online boutique is up and running, it'll take time and effort to properly market your website, generate traffic, and attract paying customers. Your ability to earn a profit will be based in large part on what products you're selling, whether there is a demand for your products, and how much competition you have. These issues are discussed in later chapters.

What Is a Luxury Product?

Luxury fashion goods are targeted at consumers at the upper end of the wealth scale. These products range from clothing and leather goods to jewelry and other accessories. Leather bags, gold watches, diamond rings, and pearls are all popular items sold online.

Of course, no product category is as indelibly linked with the affluent consumer as jewelry. And while the majority of jewelry purchases still take place in stores, greater numbers of consumers are flocking to internet retailers for these items.

The International Diamond and Jewelry Exchange (idexonline.com) and the U.S. Department of Commerce (doc.gov) report, for example, that online jewelry sales accounted for 3.9 percent of all jewelry sales in 2006. And that percentage is expected to more than double by 2010, when 8.1 percent of jewelry purchases are expected to be made on the web. In the 2006 holiday season, e-commerce sales of jewelry and watches were the top growth category at a staggering 67 percent over the year before, according to data from internet research firm comScore Inc. (comscore.com).

THE ONLINE PICTURE IN GENERAL

Online shopping is growing. According to the U.S. Census Bureau (census.gov), for the third quarter of 2007, revenues generated by online-based businesses (and the online sites of traditional retail businesses) were $34.7 billion, adjusted for seasonal variation and holiday and trading-day differences, but not for price changes. This number is up 3.6 percent from the second quarter of 2007.

Luxury products are often described as sensory goods because their aesthetic characteristics are usually best appreciated through the human senses of sight, touch, and feel. So the retail store undoubtedly plays a prominent role in the overall luxury buying experience and is one of the key elements of successful luxury retailing. Luxury goods can and are being sold online, however, thanks to the current technology and the convenience-driven online retail environment.

How E-Commerce Is Different from Traditional Retail

Although a traditional retail store can sell the same products as website, there are major differences between operating a traditional brick-and-mortar retail store and an online e-commerce website that sells luxury goods. Overall, it is much easier to start and operate a business online.

Some of the costs and drawbacks associated with operating a traditional brick-and-mortar retail store include having to purchase, lease, or rent the retail space for a storefront at a cost of hundreds or thousands of dollars per month as well as the need to hire employees and managers to staff the store.

Other drawbacks include having to purchase and maintain plenty of inventory; having to purchase store fixtures and displays, not to mention cash registers and computers; and having to remain open during set operating hours. In addition, a retail store is located in a fixed location and typically only attracts customers within a specific geographic area or region. The overall start-up costs are the tens of thousands or hundreds of thousands of dollars. There is, therefore, tremendous risk involved in opening a traditional retail store as a startup business.

Operating an online boutique on the other hand offers a wide range of benefits, including very low start-up and overhead costs; a worldwide customer base; the ability to operate 24 hours per day, 365 days per year; the ability to have a flexible work schedule for the owner and employees; and smaller inventory requirements.

In addition, the business can be operated from almost anywhere—such as from a home or a small office/warehouse location. It's relatively easy for one person to create a website that's as professional looking as a site operated by a large, well-established, multimillion-dollar company, so the playing field is

ONLINE BOUTIQUE BENEFITS

Consumers love to buy high-end items online for many reasons:

➡ *Speed*. Online shoppers love the idea that all they have to do is make a selection, enter their information, and then click a button. It's as easy as that, and all from their own computer.

➡ *Convenience*. Online shoppers love the online shopping experience vs. the alternatives of shopping at a mall store or department store. There, they are rushing to get there, fighting traffic, fighting for parking, getting jostled by crowds, and enduring pushy salespeople and long lines at the register.

➡ *Selection*. This is key. Online boutiques have the capacity to offer a much wider selection of merchandise for sale in one place than either a traditional store or a catalog. This means they can uncover some truly unique items not available anywhere else.

➡ *Value*. Because an online boutique has lower inventory and other overhead costs than a brick-and-mortar retailer, these savings can be passed on to consumers in the form of great deals on the latest merchandise—even if it is high-end, luxury goods that they are after. Everyone loves a sale, right?

➡ *Education*. The internet is the world's largest storehouse of information. For example, a consumer who is in the market for an engagement ring and wants to learn about the 4Cs of diamonds can at information sites online, or at the websites of the most reputable online jewelry stores. These sites can also answer questions about how to clean jewelry, how to judge quality, or the latest styles.

much more equal. An e-commerce website can be created and open for business in hours or days, not months, or even years; There is very low financial risk—in the hundreds or thousands of dollars.

"The reason I chose to go online instead of having a brick-and-mortar store is because I felt like the market where I live is saturated," says Jennifer Spiegelhalter, founder of AdoraBella and its website ShopAdorabella.com, which sell high-fashion clothing. "There is practically a new boutique springing up on every corner these days, and e-commerce is growing by the minute. So I felt, after much research, that this was the better choice."

Should You Shutter Your Storefront?

Some online sellers start online and never have a brick-and-mortar store, but many folks thinking about starting an online boutique already have a brick-and-mortar boutique in operation. So, if you have a storefront, should you shut it down and focus exclusively on e-retailing? Not immediately. After all, by having it both ways you have the ability to market your products in two ways, give local customers an easy way to return merchandise, and use your storefront for warehousing merchandise.

Still, might this dual-channel strategy be an unnecessary complication that forces an entrepreneur to focus on two distinctly different venues? The experts don't think so, and in fact, many point to it as the way to go forward into the next century.

There are tremendous advantages to be had by leveraging net sales with a brick-and-mortar store. Case in point: You can use the store to promote the website, for instance, by printing the URL on bags, sales slips, and advertising fliers.

In short, a brick-and-mortar store can be a billboard for your website. It already has massive brand awareness, and whenever a customer walks in, even walks by, a storefront, there's reinforcement of the URL.

Another argument in favor of a dual-channel strategy: Different consumers want different things, and you want to be open to that. Some customers want the kind of personal interaction that can only happen in a traditional retail setting. For others, it's simpler to log on to the net. The smart, consumer-oriented business makes it easy to buy, no matter the customer's preferences.

The Wonderful World of Online Boutiques

Throughout this book, you'll meet many online boutique owners. Some of the online boutique owners you'll meet in these pages include Amanda Raab,

THE E-COMMERCE QUIZ

Think you're ready to become an online boutique owner? Prove it. Before moving on to the next chapter, take this quiz. Answers are true or false.

1. I'm comfortable in a game in which tomorrow's rules are invented the day after tomorrow. __ __

2. I see inefficiencies—waste and delay—in many current business practices. __ __

3. I'm willing to delay this year's profits to potentially make more money next year. __ __

4. I know how to size up customers I've never seen or talked with. __ __

5. The net excites me; I honestly like surfing around and seeing what's new. __ __

6. I can live with thin margins. __ __

7. Customer satisfaction is the most important thing a business can deliver. __ __

8. I'm not afraid of battling titans. __ __

9. I see opportunity where others see risks. __ __

10. I am willing to work harder and smarter than I ever could have imagined possible. __ __

Scoring: Guess what? "True" is always the right answer for any netpreneur. But you knew that already because you're ready to compete on this merciless playing field.

CEO of PurePeals.com, which sells luxurious and elegant pearl jewelry at good value; Andrea Edmunds, president of PoshTots.com, which sells imaginative heirloom-quality furnishings and gifts for children; as well as Jennifer Spielgelhalter.

You'll also hear from Heather Smith, founder of Cocosshoppe.com, which sells eco-luxe fashion and beauty products; Linda Hayes, founder of Tonic Home Inc., whose website TonicHome.com sells luxury home furnishings; Jay Valentine, whose online jewelry store SaladoJewelry.com sells medium-priced jewelry; and Lisa Cabanes, whose website SocialCouture.com sells at home entertaining products and services.

Finally, look out for commentary from Kassie Remple, owner/founder of SimplySoles, whose website SimplySoles.com sells beautifully designed and expertly crafted shoes; Ali Wing, CEO and co-founder of Giggle, whose website Giggle.com sells stylish and smart baby gear; and Jacquelyn Tran, president and founder of Perfume Bay Inc. which sells cosmetics, perfume, and skin-care products on its website Perfumebay.com; and Eileen Joy Spitalny and David Kravetz of Fairytale Brownies, whose website Fairytale brownies.com, sells, you guessed it, brownies.

Throughout the book, we will also include Q and A's with successful online boutique owners. These are designed to help you see how a successful online boutique gets started and grows. While these online boutique owners are different in many ways, they all have two things in common—the drive to build online stores selling luxury goods, and success.

eBags Inc.

Peter Cobb, co-founder, senior vice president of marketing and merchandising

Location: Greenwood Village, Colorado

Year Started: 1998

Eliot and Peter Cobb, Frank Steed, and Andy Young joined Jon Nordmark in 1998 to build a major online store for shoes and accessories. Boy, have they pulled it off. Currently, eBags (ebags.com) is the world's largest online retailer of bags and accessories for all lifestyles. It has sold more than 4 million bags and accessories since the site launched in March 1999. Of the five founders, Peter Cobb and Jon Nordmark remain with the company.

eBags has grown 40 percent per month since its launch and has launched eBags in the EU, with strong sales in the United Kingdom and Germany.

The company also has a footwear and accessory site called 6PM.com (6PM.com) that has over 125 brands, 130,000 pairs of shoes, and many of the same bag brands as eBags.

The company officers are very excited about the site because it allows for much more "ensemble merchandising." eBags can show Stuart Weitzman shoes, for example, next to matching handbags or Allen Edmonds men's dress shoes with a Swiss Army laptop brief. In general, the company says it offers lots of fun opportunities to improve the shopping experience.

Steed was president of Samsonite USA and American Tourister prior to launching eBags. Peter Cobb, Young, and Nordmark were also top executives at Samsonsite. Each had product development, merchandising, and marketing experience with globally-recognized consumer brands. Eliot Cobb was formerly the vice president/treasurer of The Wherehouse, a 350-store retail music chain located on the West Coast. As a group, the Cobbs, Steed, Young, and Nordmark possessed more than 60 years of combined bag and retail experience.

To start the company in early 1998, each of the five founders came up with a significant amount of cash and worked without pay for eight months. Then eBags raised $8 million from angels, friends, and family. The company then decided it wanted to get venture capital funding, so it carved back its angel funding to $4 million and actually sent checks back to all its angels. In 1999, financial relief came from VC firm Benchmark Capital. Other investors followed, allowing eBags to continually invest in people and technology. While the company has raised a total of $30 million in VC funding, it has not needed to raise VC money since 1999.

The company is doing well. eBags.com announced the company concluded the 2007 holiday quarter with a significant increase in handbag sales, up 43 percent in the past year-over-year. More high-end, designer brand names helped eBags increase its average order size 13 percent during the holiday quarter (vs. 2006).

A key to the company's success? It does not overspend. Executives don't have golden parachutes or big bonuses. In fact, no one at the company, including its executives, makes a six-figure salary. And after 9/11, all employees, including the executives, took a 10 percent pay cut without complaint.

This kind of frugal approach is one reason eBags.com is still around when so many other dotcoms aren't.

Another success secret? eBags maintains little or no inventory of its own. Instead, it relies on manufacturers to drop-ship products directly to customers. For example, 312 of the 330 brands eBags currently sells are sent by drop-shipping, including High Sierra Sport Co., Samsonite, and Kipling. The practice has turned eBags into a luggage category killer. Its selection of over 15,000 SKUs dwarfs the several hundred items carried by the average specialty baggage store. Company executives believe this lack of inventory is one of the primary reasons eBags has survived.

Here, Peter Cobb discusses some other secrets to eBags' success.

What made you decide to launch eBags.com?

Peter Cobb: In May 1998, we saw what was going on with people starting companies selling books and music online, and there was a product we knew and loved—bags—that we knew would be a great fit for the internet. We knew from our research that many people were buying bags through catalogs, so we knew that people didn't need to feel and touch the product to make a purchase decision. They were comfortable buying bags from Orvis, L.L. Bean, Lands' End, and Eddie Bauer catalogs. We knew bags and accessories weren't like clothes or shoes, where people really needed to see the color, the size, and the materials. Also, people don't really get excited about going to the mall Saturday afternoon to pick out some luggage or a backpack for their son. So with three, four, or five photographs nicely done for a product, you can really get the point across.

Another key reason we started was because the retail bag market was very fragmented. If you wanted luggage, you'd probably go to a travel goods specialty

---

CLICK TIP

Is there a niche out there that you are familiar with that isn't on the web yet—and you just know it could be a perfect fit? Then what are you waiting for? As eBags' success shows, if you have the right niche product and you do e-tailing right, you will find success on the internet.

store. If you wanted a ladies' handbag, you'd probably go to a department store. And if you were looking for backpacks, you'd go to a sporting goods store. There was no "Bags R Us." Because of this fragmentation, we knew there'd be a great opportunity. And there happened to be nice margins on the product—markups [average] 50 percent.

The other important thing is that in the brick-and-mortar retail world, when inventory comes in, it's there for 180 days. If somebody buys a bag, the store orders another one. What's more, these stores are limited to about 250 products because of physical space.

Because we do business on the internet, however, we can offer more than 15,000 products, and when we take an order, we pass it on to Samsonite, for example, and Samsonite ships it to the customer. We get the sale and then, 30 to 120 days later, we pay the brand.

How long did it take to go from idea to funding to launch?

Cobb: Idea to funding was about eight months; idea to launch was 10 months.

What's been the biggest surprise you've had in building eBags?

Cobb: There have been a few of them. The biggest surprise is how we've been able to gain such fantastic momentum. We've shipped 6.8 million bags.

Another one probably has been watching the flameout of all the e-tailers that took in many times more money than we did and somehow spent it all. It's been a huge surprise to see companies that I thought were pretty solid companies [fail]—like eToys, Garden.com, and MotherNature.com, sites I shopped on and had great shopping experiences with. What you don't know, however, is what is going on behind the scenes. These companies were spending tens of millions of dollars on inventory in their warehouses, which we didn't have to do. They were also spending money on television advertising, which we never really did. We have a saying at eBags: "Too much money makes you stupid." We just kept seeing that over and over again. We didn't raise nearly as much money as these guys did, and we always understood that the money we were dealing with was our money— money we put into the company with some investors' help. Every decision we made was "This is our money; how should we spend it?" as opposed to

"Boy, we've got $80 million in the bank, so who cares if we spend $1 million on Super Bowl ads?"

Another surprise has been how much internet retailing has taken hold with a large percentage of the population. I think it has mainstreamed. I've heard numbers like 67 percent of the population bought something online during last year's holiday season and the growth of broadband has made online shopping faster and more enjoyable. I think that says good things for the future of internet retailing for those who are doing it right.

What's been your biggest challenge?

Cobb: I think the biggest challenge is managing your cash properly while continuing to grow.

How many VCs did you meet with before you got a funding commitment?

Cobb: We met with well over 100 VC firms.

What's your strategy in coming out ahead of competitors?

Cobb: Our competition is really brick-and-mortar stores. Online shopping isn't for everybody. Some people want to feel and touch and taste and smell before they buy a product, and that's OK. But a large majority of shoppers value convenience and selection, and that's why online shopping is experiencing explosive growth. Bags and accessories is a $30 billion market. Our strategy is just to continue to offer the ultimate shopping experience on eBags.com.

ONLINE LUXURY ITEM LIST

Here is a list of important things to keep in mind when selling your luxury items online. Clip it out and keep it taped to your computer. You should always be thinking about your customers.

1. *Stellar customer service*. Consumers may take advantage of shopping online in order to avoid salespeople, but what if they want to ask a question or change

---

ONLINE LUXURY ITEM LIST, CONTINUED

their mind about a selection they made? Does your online boutique have a telephone number where they can speak to customer service? If so, what hours are they available (be sure to verify time zones)?

2. *Clear information*. Make sure you have clear information on guarantees, secure ordering, lost/damaged shipments, and returns. A piece of jewelry, leather handbag, or one-of-a-kind piece of baby furniture is a major investment, and consumers want to be sure your purchase is guaranteed and that their purchase price can be refunded if they to return the item.

3. *Good shipping choices*. Consumers want to know that the online boutique they are doing business with—as well as their suppliers—ship using insured carriers such as FedEx and UPS and that all shipments are insured for the full value of their contents. Be sure to do this.

4. *Clear images*. If a shopper finds a product that interests them, make sure they can click its image to make it larger so they can get a better look. While this is not necessarily a good substitute for seeing the piece in person, it will give them a pretty good idea of what the piece looks like.

5. *Have secure transactions*. Today, most online boutiques guarantee that all personal information consumers provide for payment or registration purposes is automatically encrypted by the latest security software. It eliminates the risk of data interception, manipulation, or recipient impersonation by unauthorized parties. Consumers want this security, so make sure you give it to them.

6. *Have a privacy policy*. Most online boutiques today that collect any personal data (even an e-mail address) have their privacy policy posted. Consumers review these privacy policies to confirm that their private information will not be sold to other companies, specifically marketing companies or partners with similar products. So make sure you don't do this.

Chapter 1

Getting Started

*N*ow that you are ready to enter the world of online boutiques and luxury goods, its time to take a step back and think about some important things you'll need to do before actually getting started—and that includes writing a business plan and getting funding. The first six chapters of this book will cover everything you will be able to do in one week. The rest focuses on helping you develop and grow your business, including how to set up your business, legal issues to be aware of, and resources you'll need to help you set up your business's infrastructure.

Sounds Like a Plan

Within the first week of planning your online boutique, it is imperative that you write your e-business plan. You are most likely exploring new territory, making decisions about technology and marketing, and establishing a new set of vendor relationships, so a well-thought-out plan gives you guidance.

The first step in writing an e-business plan is deciding what kind of experience you want your online customers to have. Think not only about today but also about two and five years down the road. Your e-commerce plan starts with website goals. Who are your target customers? What do they need? Are they getting information only, or can they buy products at your site? These key questions, asked and answered early, will determine how much time and money you'll need to develop and maintain an online presence.

Second, decide what products or services you will offer. How will you position and display them? Will you offer both online and offline purchasing? How will you handle shipping and returns? Additionally, don't overlook the customer's need to reach a live person.

As you explore the web for vendors to support your e-business, have a clear idea of how you want to handle the "back end" of the business. If you decide to sell online, you will need a shopping cart program, a means of handling credit card information, and a fulfillment process. However, you may decide that your site is informational only and that you will continue to process transactions offline. These are all important business decisions.

CLICK TIP

Need help writing your online boutique business plan? Try Business Plan Pro software (bplans.com) from Palo Alto Software Inc. The software has more than 500 business plan templates that you can quickly customize to match your business. Or you can use the software's step-by-step wizard to easily create a custom business plan from scratch.

CLICK TIP

If you're serious about the success of your online business, then you need to find ways to give yourself every advantage you can over your competition. One way is building a customized blueprint that outlines exactly how your businesses will succeed. Remember: The process of writing a business plan for your company can be a crucial step in getting your profits to where you want them to be.

The last important decision is your promotional strategy, which gets even more important when you think about the millions of websites out there. Remember: The promotional strategy for your website is no less important than the promotional strategy for your business as a whole.

Getting Funding

One of the beauties of starting an e-business today is that it doesn't take a lot of money to start it. In fact, statistics from the Small Business Administration indicate that about $6,000 is what's required to start the average business today.

Most online boutique owners do the following to finance themselves: They bootstrap their business using their own money.

Financial bootstrapping is a term used to cover different methods for avoiding using the financial resources of external investors. The use of private credit cards is the most known form of bootstrapping, but a wide variety of methods are available for entrepreneurs. For example, entrepreneurs thinking of bootstrapping their business can also take out second mortgages or tap into their personal savings.

While bootstrapping involves a risk—especially if you are not a millionaire—the absence of any other stakeholder gives you more freedom to develop the company the way you want to do it. Many successful companies including Dell Computers were founded this way.

SBA LOANS

Some online boutique owners turn to the U.S. Small Business Administration for loans to start their businesses.

In general, all SBA loan programs lend to small businesses unable to secure financing on reasonable terms through normal lending channels.

The loan programs are operated through private-sector lenders that provide loans which are, in turn, guaranteed by the SBA. Most private lenders (banks, credit unions, etc.) are familiar with SBA loan programs so interested applicants should contact their local lender for further information and assistance in the SBA loan application process.

Here is a brief description of the some loan programs available through funding from the SBA.

➡ *7(a) Loan Guaranty Program*. One of the SBA's primary loan programs, 7(a) offers loans of up to $2,000,000. (The maximum dollar amount the SBA can guaranty is generally $1 million.)

➡ *Microloan Program*. This program offers loans of up to $35,000 to qualified start-up, newly established, or growing small business concerns. Loans are arranged through nonprofit community-based lenders (intermediaries) which, in turn, make loans to eligible borrowers.

➡ *Targeted Loan Programs*. Besides the general programs described above, the SBA offers several loans designed to meet specific needs.

➡ *Other SBA Loans*. For complete information on the loan programs shown above, as well as other more specialized loans available through the SBA, see www.sba.org.

When You Need Lots of Money

Sometimes bootstrapping is not enough. Or, sometimes, your own money won't cover the expenses you need to start your online boutique.

When this is the case, there are three places you can turn: friends and family; angel investors; and venture capitalists (VCs).

Friends and Family

This seems an obvious choice. There are

CLICK TIP

Want to see the definitive top ten list for starting a business? Then check out StartupNation's "Ten Steps to Open for Business" at startupnation.com/steps/55/10-steps-open-start-business.htm. It will give you a top ten list covering everything you'll need to open a business.

people who believe in you. The downside: If you fail you still have to live with them. The upside: If you succeed, then they will share your success.

But with loved ones, you've got to structure any financing for your small business very carefully—and understand that the future of the relationship may ride on the success of your new venture. After all, there are good reasons why some people call this form of business financing the "family, friends, and fools" approach.

Before knocking down mom and dad's door, make sure you understand their motives. After all, while the vast majority of family and friends who will contribute financially to your startup are motivated mainly by the desire to help you out—another motivating factor could be that they see your small business as a decent investment. Either way, it's crucial for you to understand their motivations, because it will appropriately color how you approach obtaining business financing from them.

The folks at StartupNation also recommend giving a "kitchen-table" pitch to family and friends. What is this? It's basically a pitch that you would give to investors. Load up your presentation with newspaper articles and other things that underscore the potential market you're describing to them, and provide them with a copy of your business plan.

Also, from the get-go, make sure everyone understands that you are just getting a loan and that you're going to pay it back—it's not an equity investment.

Then, formulate a repayment plan that lines up with your business plan, and come up with a reasonable and easy-to-understand interest rate. Put the plan on paper, maybe even get a lawyer's help in drafting it. But make the schedule friendly to yourself and your venture.

Once you've settled on a repayment plan, you (or your attorney) should draft an official loan agreement to protect both parties and ensure that everyone understands this is business, not personal.

Finally, do a gut check before going ahead. Are you going to be able to fulfill the promises that you made to all of your hopeful supporters? Is everyone clear on the amount, timing, and circumstances of repayment? If your small business fails, can you still not only look them in the eye but also break bread harmoniously once again? If you can't answer a resounding yes to each of these questions, you might want to go back to the drawing board.

Angel Investing

Another alternative to venture capital funding is angel investors. Angel investors are individuals who invest in companies at an early stage in exchange for equity and the chance to help guide the company. In contrast, venture capitalists invest as a profession and generally on behalf of other investors.

Generally, people are ready to approach angels when they have exhausted their friends and family's funding but are not yet ready to approach venture capitalists for money. They are looking for large amounts ($25,000 to $1 million) of start money. The people who provide angel funding have already made it big in their own careers and can help guide you to do the same. The

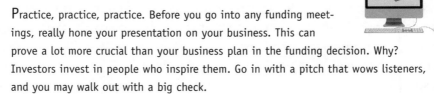

CLICK TIP

Practice, practice, practice. Before you go into any funding meetings, really hone your presentation on your business. This can prove a lot more crucial than your business plan in the funding decision. Why? Investors invest in people who inspire them. Go in with a pitch that wows listeners, and you may walk out with a big check.

CLICK TIP

It is not always easy to find VCs and angel investors because many choose to be anonymous for obvious reasons. They would always have people knocking at their door wanting to borrow money. The best way to find them is to network. In short, talk to everyone you know because you never know who they might know. In addition, keep in mind that the internet is also an infinite source of information.

pros of working with angels include the fact that they invest more than money. They provide mentoring and contacts; they are patient about their investment; and there are no monthly payments with this type of financing. Angels make their money when you achieve your business's exit strategy.

The downside, however, is that angels are difficult to find and require regular and thorough reporting, which can take up valuable time. In addition, as with VCs, you are giving up equity in your company.

Venturing into Venture Capital Funding

Venture capitalists are individuals or companies with large amounts of capital to invest and who expect higher returns. They typically only invest in established companies.

Experts say you should only use venture capitalists if you already have a great track record in your field or as an entrepreneur and if you have a business concept that requires a lot of money ($250,000 to millions) and will have a rapid growth curve. They also say that when getting funding from a VC firm, you must be willing to give up significant control over major decisions for your company; have a fast-growth company; and have an aggressive exit strategy to sell your business or do an IPO within five to seven years.

If, by chance, you go decide to go the VC route, what should you do first? For starters, in your e-business plan for your online boutique pay very close attention to the possible payday ahead (typically this is made vivid with charts that forecast revenue and profits). In short, an idea has to have the clear potential to be a major winner.

VENTURE EXPERTS

Want a source to tap for timely, practical information on how to start, manage, and expand your business? Try Kauffman eVenturing (eVenturing.org), a website from the Ewing Marion Kauffman Foundation, a Kansas City, Missouri-based private, nonpartisan foundation that works with partners to advance entrepreneurship in America.

Kauffman eVenturing offers a guide to entrepreneurs on the fast-paced journey toward high growth. The site offers rich content, including articles created by entrepreneurs exclusively for the site and an in-depth aggregation of existing information on the web on a wide array of subjects—from accessing capital to implementing successful recruiting strategies and competing in global markets. The site also features fresh material every day, gathered though a link-blog that Kauffman has established to identify the latest information on different aspects of entrepreneurship from a wide variety of sources.

The Kauffman eVenturing site is organized around six subject areas: finance, human resources, sales and marketing, products/services, operations, and the entrepreneur (e.g., strategy, culture, leadership). New collections of articles are featured once a month, rotating among those subjects. The site is very easy to search and navigate, so entrepreneurs can find the information they need quickly. Keywords in every article are tagged so that available information about a specific query can be assembled immediately.

VCs want big winners because they're realists who know that out of every ten ventures they fund, maybe eight will vanish without a trace; one will be a modest success; and one will be a home run, but that one home run will generate so much cash, it will make all the losses forgettable as it propels the firm deep into black ink. So don't be conservative. Think big.

Next, think of the exit strategy. That's key. VCs don't invest to hold; they want a way to translate a business success into an economic success. Usually, that means the company gets bought by a big fish or goes public. Either way, early investors want to know how they will get out of this deal before they go into it.

Once you have your plan in hand—with an exit strategy and a payday spelled out—you look for every way possible to get it (and yourself) in front of VCs. It isn't easy. So often internet entrepreneurs complain, "I have a great business plan, and nobody will fund it." Maybe the plan is great, maybe it isn't, but step one in proving you've got what it takes to prosper in the rugged internet economy is finding a way to get in front of VCs.

You've tried and can't seem to land VC money? Take what cash you can from anybody, of course. Get the business afloat. Then maybe VCs will come calling with cash in their hands. Even better, once a business is prospering, you can usually get much more favorable terms from VCs. The earlier they come in, the bigger piece of the company they want, which means second-stage VC financing may actually be more desirable.

The moral: When the idea is good, the money will follow.

Cashman Computer Associates
DBA Moon River Pearls

Peter L. Cashman, chairman/CEO and co-founder
(with son Bob Cashman and John Ekegren)

Location: Old Lyme, Connecticut

Year started: 2004

Want to learn some pearls of e-commerce wisdom? Then meet Peter L. Cashman, chairman/CEO of Cashman Computer Associates, which provides IT outsourcing and support for small to medium companies in New England. CCA also does business as Moon River Pearls. Its website, moonriver pearls.com, sells classic and modern pearl jewelry.

Prior to CCA, Cashman was chairman and co-founder of Environmental Data Resources Inc, an e-commerce environmental information services company, and CEO of Sanborn Map Company, acquired by EDR in 1996. The enterprise was sold in 1999 to the Daily Mail and General Trust PLC, of London.

Having successfully sold EDR and bored with retirement, in 2000, Peter was introduced to the idea of e-commerce by his son Bob, who encouraged him to take a look at a new business model for Bob's company, Cashman Computer Associates LLC (Peter eventually became chairman/CEO).

Bob proposed that CCA put the company's internet technology talents and web hosting infrastructure to work creating e-commerce websites in partnership with small ongoing direct mail businesses and/or create a new business selling profitable specialty products on the internet. "Not surprisingly, the e-commerce idea was the result of listening to our customers, something that we pride ourselves on as we go about our daily activities providing on-site IT consulting services," says Bob.

Bob says one of these customers had launched a very successful teen clothing site in 2003 and a silver jewelry site in 2004. "I could see no reason that CCA, given our staff and IT focus, could not provide e-commerce services to existing sites or whole new businesses," he says.

Peter says the key to launching the new business was finding the right product. The criteria were straightforward: The product had to be appealing, have high margins, and because of the need to ship worldwide, be lightweight.

With these criteria in mind, Peter began a series of lunches, phone calls, and meetings with a long list of friends, acquaintances, and former business associates he had met over 35 years. His search ultimately led to John Ekegren. "I have known John, a graduate of West Point and a phenomenal mechanical engineer, for many years," Peter says. "I knew he had been involved with trade between the United States and China but I did not know that he served on the board of a Chinese manufacturing company and that he typically traveled to China at least four times a year."

"At lunch," Peter continues, "I learned that a Chinese businessman who served on a board with John had once told John that if he ever wanted to sell pearl jewelry in the States, he had a great source in China." One thing led to another and the future partners became very serious about this opportunity.

To assess the competition, CCA purchased pearls from the top ten pearl websites and evaluated every aspect of their product, price, packaging, site design, guarantee, return policy, and service.

"That evaluation," Peter says, "convinced us we could be a successful niche player. We agreed that John's company, PTI, would supply the jewelry from China and provide shipping, handling, and customer service and that CCA would build, maintain, own and operate the e-commerce web store." Bob says, "Our goal is to offer the best value in classic pearl jewelry available on the internet. We believe we have accomplished that objective." Peter says that it took six months of heroic effort by the combined staff of PTI and CCA to be ready for business in December 2004.

The site offers a convenient, simple approach to buying great gifts for any occasion. Peter says that Moon River's jewelry sells for a fraction of the cost of retail, ships free via UPS, comes with a 30-day money-back guarantee, and arrives in an elegant gift box. In coming months, the Cashmans plan to add Tahitian pearls, gemstone and silver jewelry from India, and unique designer items to the site. Read more about Cashman's success story below.

What were your startup costs?

Peter Cahsman: Nominal. We had all the programming staff and IT infrastructure in-house. The learning curve was steep, but we did add two new staff for this project at a total cost of roughly $150,000.

What are your monthly revenues?

Cashman: Annual revenues are growing at two times over last year, and we anticipate sales in excess of $500,000 this year.

What are your monthly visitor counts?

Cashman: In excess of 20,000.

How do you attract visitors?

Cashman: Pay-per-click and a major effort to win the search engine battle, which is a big deal. Viral marketing is also huge for us. Twenty-five percent of our business comes from repeat buyers, which in the online jewelry business is fantastic. So getting folks to the site is job number one. Job number two is converting them to customers. Once they experience our customer service, they will come back!

What are your secrets of success?

Cashman: Smart people who work damn hard.

What were some of the most difficult challenges you had starting out?

Cashman: We underestimated how difficult search engine optimization could be, and it took time to get enough product on the site to be meaningful.

What advice would you give e-commerce entrepreneurs just starting out?

Cashman: If you don't have capital, you can start small if you are patient, willing to learn, and work 24 hours, seven days a week. Customer service is also a huge component of success, so remember that it will chew up a ton of time. Finally, it goes without saying you need a quality product offered at a compelling price.

CLICK TIP

Peter Cashman says the key to launching a new business is finding the right product. For Cashman, that meant an appealing, lightweight product that had high margins. Pearls, of course. Remember that not every product is right for online selling. So before you decide to break into the world of e-commerce, make sure you have the right product to sell and an ample product supply. Hey, you never know. It could be the next big thing.

Setting Up Your Business

Next, we'll discuss how to actually set up your business.

Legal Structure

When setting up your online boutique, one of the first things you will need to do is choose the legal structure for it. Aside from being necessary for government reporting and tax purposes, this can enable your business to operate more efficiently.

In general, your business can be a sole proprietorship, a partnership, or a corporation. Each has advantages and disadvantages depending on the type of activity you are engaged in. Your goal is to choose the form that works best for you.

Sole Proprietorship

A business owned by one person, who is entitled to all of its profits and responsible for all of its debts, is considered a sole proprietorship. This legal form is the simplest, providing maximum control and minimum government interference. Currently used by more than 75 percent of all businesses, it is often the suggested way for a new business that does not carry great personal liability threats. The owner simply needs to secure the necessary licenses, tax identification numbers, and certifications in his or her name, and you are now in business

The main advantages that differentiate the sole proprietorship from the other legal forms are the ease with which it can be started; the owner's freedom to make decisions; and the distribution of profits (owner takes all).

Still, the sole proprietorship is not without disadvantages, the most serious of which is its unlimited liability. As a sole proprietor, you are responsible for all business debts. Should these exceed the assets of your business, your creditors can claim your personal assets—home, automobile, savings account, and investments. Sole proprietorships also tend to have more difficulty obtaining capital and holding on to key employees. This stems from the fact that sole proprietorships generally have fewer resources and offer less opportunity for job advancement. Thus, anyone who chooses sole proprietorship should be prepared to be a generalist, performing a variety of functions, from accounting to advertising.

Partnership

A business owned by two or more people, who agree to share in its profits, is considered a partnership. Like the sole proprietorship, it is easy to start and the red tape involved is usually minimal. The tax structure is the same as proprietorship except in the profits and losses of the partnership are divided by an agreed percentage by the partners.

The main advantages of the partnership form are that the business can draw on the skills and abilities of each partner; offer employees the opportunity to become partners; and utilize the partners' combined financial resources.

However, for your own protection, it is advisable to have a written agreement that will spell out the specifics of the partnership. This should state each partner's rights and responsibilities; the amount of capital each partner is investing in the business; the distribution of profits; what happens if a partner joins or leaves the business; and how the assets are to be divided if the business is discontinued. Things have a way of changing and people forgetting over time, so it is essential that there be a signed document that all abide by.

Partnerships also have disadvantages. The unlimited liability that applies to sole proprietorships is even worse for partnerships. As a partner, for example, you are responsible not only for your own business debts, but for those of your partners as well. Should they incur debts or legal judgments against the business, you could be held legally responsible for them. Disputes among partners can be a problem, too. Unless you and your partners see eye to eye on how the business should be run and what it should accomplish, you are in for trouble.

In general, many experts believe a partnership is generally the least advisable way to go. It requires filing a separate partnership tax return, does not carry liability protection for general partners, and can lead into legal and personal disputes. A corporate form of ownership is generally recognized as preferable over partnership, because it can serve the same purpose while offering a cleaner and better protected structure for the owners.

Corporation

A corporation differs from the other legal forms of business in that the law regards it as an artificial being possessing the same rights and responsibilities as a person.

This means that, unlike sole proprietorships or partnerships, it has an existence separate from its owners. It has all the legal rights of an individual in regards to conducting commercial activity—it can sue, be sued, own property, sell property, and sell the rights of ownership in the form of exchanging stock for money.

As a result, the corporation offers some unique advantages. This includes limited liability: owners are not personally responsible for the debts of the business. Other advantages are the ability to raise capital by selling shares of stock and easy transfer of ownership from one individual to another. Plus, unlike the sole proprietorship and partnership, the corporation has "unlimited life" and thus the potential to outlive its original owners.

The main disadvantage of the corporate form can be summed up in two words: taxation and complexity. In what amounts to double taxation, you must pay taxes on both the income the corporation earns and the income you earn as an individual. Along with this, corporations are required to pay an annual tax on all outstanding shares of stock.

Given its complexity, a corporation is both more difficult and more expensive to start than are the sole proprietorship and the partnership. In order to form a corporation, you must be granted a charter by the state in which your e-boutique is located. For a small business, the cost of incorporating usually ranges from $500 to $1,500. This includes the costs for legal assistance in drawing up your charter, state incorporation fees, and the purchase of record books and stock certificates.

And, since corporations are subject to closer regulation by the government, the owners must bear the ongoing cost of preparing and filing state and federal reports.

S Corporation

If you are interested in forming a corporation, but hesitate to do so because of the double taxation, there is a way to avoid it. You can do this by making your business an S corporation. The Internal Revenue Service (IRS) permits this type of corporation to be taxed as a partnership rather than a corporation. However, in order to qualify for S status, your business must meet the specific requirements set forth by the IRS. These include limits on the number and type of shareholders in the business; the stock that is issued; and the corporation's sources of revenues.

CLICK TIP

To learn more about forming a corporation, visit mycorporation.com or incorporate.com. These are independent companies that can help you inexpensively complete the necessary paperwork and establish a corporation or LLC quickly. Your lawyer or accountant can also help with this process.

No matter which you choose, there is paperwork to fill out and fees to pay in order to obtain local, state and federal business licenses that may be required.

To learn more about forming a corporation, visit mycorporation.com or incorporate.com. These are independent companies that can help you inexpensively complete the necessary paperwork and establish a corporation quickly. Your lawyer or accountant can also help with this process.

The laws and fees for establishing a corporation vary by state, as do the benefits (legal and financial) for establishing this type of business entity. The type of legal entity you establish will also impact your personal and business tax liabilities in the future.

Choosing a Name for Your Business

Another important step is choosing a name for your business. Once the name is selected, you'll want to register your online business's domain name (website address), and you might want to have a company logo designed. Depending on the business name and the unique look of your logo, it may be advisable to copyright and/or trademark your company's name and logo. This is something you can do yourself, or hire a lawyer to do on your behalf. More on choosing a domain name can be found in Chapter 4.

CLICK TIP

To learn more about copyrights and trademarks, visit the United States Patent and Trademark Office's website at uspto.gov. The United States Copyright Office's website can be found at copyright.gov. The forms you'll need to file your patents, trademarks, and copyrights, as well as directions and fees for doing this can be found on these websites.

Money Matters

After consulting with your financial planner or accountant and establishing your business, you'll probably want to set up a separate business checking account. Visit with several banks and financial institutions to shop around for a bank that offers the most services for the lowest fees.

Depending on the turnkey website and e-commerce solution you wind up using, you may also need to obtain a credit card merchant account from a bank or financial institution, which allows you to accept credit and debit card payments online or over the telephone. Some of the turnkey solutions described later in this book handle credit card processing on your behalf, so obtaining your own merchant account won't be necessary.

LEGAL EAGLES

Covering your legal bases is perhaps one of the most important things to consider when starting up your online boutique. If you don't pay enough attention to the legal aspects of your web business, you could end up in litigation or lose valuable assets such as your logo, brand, or site itself.

Unlike setting up shop in the real world, on the web all the assets you purchase, create, own, and operate to generate business and revenue consist of intellectual property rights, such as copyrights, trademarks, patents, and trade secrets. As a result, you will have to align yourself with a reputable lawyer, preferably one that understands intellectual property rights and the internet.

When you meet with your lawyer for the first time, you'll probably discuss the basics, such as who the founders of your company are and what type of company it is—and then delve into trademark issues, such as whether or not you've checked them properly, and the importance of protecting them. You'll hopefully also get into copyright law, patent law, libel law, individual privacy law, and trade secret law.

Trade secret law is particularly important for internet companies that have a new and valuable concept no other company has. In general, the law states that everyone who

LEGAL EAGLES, CONTINUED

has access to your ideas agree in writing to a confidentiality agreement that says they will not disclose them or use them themselves, then the law will protect your ideas. A good confidentiality agreement should be signed by all of your employees, independent contractors, and even investors. It should be drafted in the very early stages of the startup.

The legalities don't end there. It's also a good idea for companies that use web development firms to develop their sites to be aware of ownership issues. In short, internet merchants need to make sure that they, not the developer, own their website, and they have the right to use and make any changes to the site.

How do you find the right lawyer? Use your contacts, or try FindLaw (findlaw.com), a website that not only offers names of law firms (organized by region) that specialize in specific issues but also lawyers that cater to small business. You can also access much legal information on Findlaw that can help you run your e-business.

Your Business's Infrastructure

Putting together all of the pieces for your business's infrastructure before you go online and start selling products is essential. If you're not sure how to proceed with any of these initial steps, seek guidance from experienced accountants, lawyers, consultants, and other business professionals. A free source of business advice is SCORE (score.org), which has volunteer (mostly retired) business professionals willing to offer advice and guidance to first-time business operators and entrepreneurs. SCORE's website offers free online tools and resources of interest to new business operators.

The U.S. Small Business Administration's website (sba.gov) is another excellent source for free, online tools and information of interest to anyone starting a small business. The Small Business Planner section of this site will take you step-by-step through the process of establishing the infrastructure of your new business.

Another free, online resource for new online boutique owners is Entrepre neur.com, which is maintained by the publisher of *Entrepreneur* magazine and Entrepreneur Press. Click on the "Starting a Business" and "E-Business" icons on the site's homepage to start learning about how to establish your business. The site also offers marketing and advertising tutorials and advice.

Once your business's infrastructure is in place, you're ready to start developing your website and marketing your products.

Chapter 2

How to Choose the Products You'll Sell

*A*s we discussed in the introduction, the focus here is on luxury products, higher-end products than you see in a traditional online store. So we focus on fashion (clothes and accessories), jewelry (pearls and other types of jewelry), housewares, gifts, and baby items, among others.

But what kinds of luxury products should you sell? For example, if you are selling high-end clothing, should you sell women's clothing? Men's clothing? Children's clothing? A specific type of clothing, such as women's lingerie or handmade baby products? Of course, you can also decide to sell everything in your fashion store.

Another choice that you have is whose clothing, jewelry, or merchandise to sell. If you also enjoy designing and making your own clothing or fashion accessories, you may want to sell your own designs. It's more likely, of course, that you will sell the work of other fashion designers or jewelry makers. As an online boutique owner, you should be able to find clothing designers or manufacturers who are willing to sell their clothing and clothing accessories to you at affordable prices.

A key consideration in deciding what product to sell is what your existing competition in cyberspace is selling. As you probably already know, there is a good chance that you'll find competitive websites offering identical or similar luxury products to those you're thinking about selling.

"While we grapple with some of the usual challenges of having an online boutique, such as internet fraud and handling credit card vendors, the biggest issue we have by far is finding products that do not have any other web outlet," says Jay Valentine of Saladojewelry.com. "The single largest issue is how to find items that are not all over the place."

Setting Yourself Apart

You need to set your website and its products apart and determine what added to offer.

Valentine says that he has been able to overcome the uniqueness issue somewhat by seeking products in international locations. "We found that going to places like Ireland, Italy, Sardinia, and Sicily, as well as meeting with jewelry artists who had no web presence, worked best," says Valentine, who adds that his site does sell Pandora, a national line, which is widely available elsewhere online. "But, the difference is that when people come to our website, they cross-buy many other items that are indeed unique."

Other ways Valentine distinguishes himself from the competition include: an easy-to-use website, lots of cross-selling, a personal note inside every box, and online event each year where special customers are invited back with special offers. But more about these techniques later.

CLICK TIP

Once you pinpoint a product you might be interested in selling, tap your skills as a web surfer and search for websites and companies that are currently selling the same or similar products. Discover who your online-based competition is or will be. Use search engines, such as Google and Yahoo!, and enter a range of different search phrases (using product names, product categories, product descriptions, and company names). Also, be sure to check shopping and price comparison websites, such as nextag.com as well as online mass-market retailers, such as Amazon.com. As you discover who your competition is, spend time surfing its websites to determine how you might do things better or differently.

PoshTots is another online boutique that prides itself on having products that sets it apart. "Our strategy was to find the most whimsical, elegant, and unique baby products around," says PoshTots.com's Andrea Edmunds. "We went against the mold at the time and offered custom-made products with extended lead times. Because the majority of our line was custom-made to order, we were able to offer options that a typical e-tailer or retailer could not offer. Customers were willing to wait longer for a custom piece of furniture."

Edmunds says that because she did not have inventory, "we did not have the initial upfront costs of buying product, inventory, and shipping costs. Our manufacturers shipped directly to our customers and invoiced us afterwards." Edmunds adds that because the margins on furniture is so much higher, "We had fewer transactions and larger per order than most e-tailers competing for the market with low prices and quick shipping."

Your Inventory Requirements

How much inventory must you maintain in-house in order to process and ship your orders within days of receiving them? If you'll be selling high-ticket items, can you initially afford to maintain the level of inventory you'll need? These are questions you, as online boutique owner, must keep top of mind. Once you determine how much inventory you'll need on-hand at any given time, you must then focus on the accessibility of that inventory. How long will

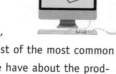

CLICK TIP

As you do your product research, keep a written list of the most common questions people have about the product. You'll want to address these questions on your online boutique's website and in marketing materials.

it take you to establish and then replenish your inventory as needed?

If an item must be imported from overseas or manufactured from scratch, this process could take weeks or months. If you'll be purchasing inventory directly from a wholesaler, manufacturer, or distributor, what will happen if your product becomes back ordered and unavailable? Will you be able to acquire the products elsewhere at a competitive price?

Can you purchase your inventory in sufficient quantities to qualify for discounts to keep your costs low? Is there a sufficient quantity of the items available to you to meet the demands of your customers? One of the worst and most costly mistakes you can make is marketing a product, generating a significant demand for it, and then not being able to fulfill your orders

CLICK TIP

Keep in mind that some online boutique owners get so excited about a new product that they order entirely too much at one time. Excess inventory creates extra overhead, and that costs you money. Inventory that sits in your garage or warehouse doesn't generate sales or profits. Newbie online boutique owners sometimes add financial insult to injury by marking overstocks at reduced prices, hoping for a quick sale. This solves the overstock problem but plays havoc with your bottom line because that product you've written into your financial plan as selling at $100 is now pulling in only $50. It's not holding up its share of the weight. You may be tempted to bounce back from this problem by getting timid with your next orders. Don't do this, either. When you reduce normal reordering, you risk creating a stock shortage, and that's not healthy for your bottom line.

So, what should you do? For starters, do as much research as you can before ordering so that you can order as realistically as possible; then order only what you feel confident will sell; and finally, establish a realistic safety margin.

2 / HOW TO CHOOSE THE PRODUCTS YOU'LL SELL

because you can't get your hands on an ample inventory supply. So when calculating your inventory needs, be sure to order enough so you don't sell out prematurely and have to turn customers away.

You may also choose not to have any inventory, as Edmunds explained above.

Pricing

Next, we will discuss cost and pricing. It is important for online boutique owners to understand that cost is a large component of pricing, as vital as competition. The ideal cost formula for a successful online boutique? That would be to purchase or acquire your inventory for the absolute lowest cost-per-unit possible and then resell those products at the highest retail price possible in order to generate a profit. That rarely happens.

No matter what quantity you're buying in, always know what your cost-per-unit is so you can make sure there's enough profit margin to cover all of your operating expenses (including your own salary and the cost of operating your website, for example). As you determine your costs, be sure to calculate in shipping charges, sales taxes (if applicable), order processing fees, warehousing costs, packaging costs, finance charges (interest, etc.), and any other expenses that will diminish your profit margins.

Some business operators rely on credit to acquire the inventory needed. Whether you use credit terms from your supplier or use a credit card to purchase inventory, chances are you'll need to pay finance charges and interest, so calculate these additional fees into your unit pricing.

You'll discover in most cases that, when acquiring inventory, you'll receive the best prices when you seek out quantity discounts. Depending on the product, this might mean ordering dozens, hundreds, or even thousands of the same product or products at once in order to benefit from the savings being offered by a manufacturer, wholesaler, or distributor. When placing larger orders, shipping and warehousing costs go up, so be prepared to do some number crunching to determine what's best for your business. Depending on what you'll be selling and who you're acquiring your inventory from, don't be afraid to negotiate for the best pricing, especially if you're purchasing a significant quantity of an item.

Cost and Pricing

Price refers to how much you'll be able to sell your products for to the customers shopping on your website. Your pricing must cover all of your expenses, allow you to generate as profit, but at the same time, be competitive (based on your competition).

As you'll discover, finding the perfect price point at which to sell your items is a process, and it may require some experimentation. In some cases, you may discover you're able to charge a premium for your products because of strong demand and limited supply in the marketplace. In other situations, you may find it necessary to discount your items or offer incentives (like free shipping) in order to compete with your competition and attract customers.

Throughout this process, it's essential that you have a firm grasp on all of your costs and your cost-per-unit so that you can ensure that your company operates in the black. After all, a wide range of factors and unexpected or hidden costs can impact your profit margins.

A less tangible cost that startup online business operators don't always take into account is the value of their time and how much of a time investment is needed to establish and launch their business, handle the day-to-day operations of the business, and ultimately fill each and every order. When all is said and done, your business should be able to generate enough profit so your "take-home pay" compensates you for this time investment. Ultimately, your pricing must reflect all of your costs and expenses.

Again, once you calculate all of your costs (based on projections) in advance, set your pricing, and do some number crunching based on projected sales, you may discover that the products you wanted to sell do not provide a viable opportunity after all.

Competition and Pricing

When it comes to pricing, PurePearls.com's Amanda Raab uses several factors, including market value, online competition, and cost. "In the jewelry market, costs change quite often because pearls come from a living organism," Raab says. "Harvest may be good some years and bad others, so costs fluctuate. Also, gold prices change everyday. These are all things that have to be taken into consideration."

One of the biggest mistakes you can make when selling luxury products online is focusing exclusively on offering the lowest price possible for your products. Although you'll be able to undercut your competition in the short-term, there will always be a competitor who can offer even lower prices. Plus, this dramatically cuts your profit margins. With lower profits, you'll earn less money for yourself, and you probably won't earn the money needed to properly market and grow your business in the future.

"Pricing is uber-important, and it is necessary to understand how to build margin into your offerings while keeping your prices competitive," says Social Couture's Lisa Cabanes. "It is too easy to get priced out of a sale if you are too greedy, and it is conversely too easy to 'work for free' if your pricing is too aggressive."

What's more, depending on the product, people may be willing to pay extra if you offer superior customer service, if you have an easy-to-use website that makes ordering easy, or if you somehow add value to what you're offering. People will also pay a premium for hard-to-find high-end products.

For Saladojewelry.com's Valentine, his pricing is based on the company's desire to sell to a very specific client—women between 27 and 58, most of whom work, have children, and earn less than $85,000 gross family income, are interested in accessories, and already own jewelry from lines like Yurman and Constantino. "As a result, we want items retailing around $40 and going up to $1,500," he says. "We have some sales above that but we are aiming at the person who wants something very unique without straining the budget. We feel very strongly about this, particularly in times of looming recession or high gas prices. Jewelry is the most discretionary sale so you cannot aim at the high end of the market." Valentine adds: "An online boutique does best when there is no risk in a transaction. In our case, people accept they can buy jewelry before touching it because of our price points."

For PoshTots' Edmunds, many of her prices are set by her manufacturers. "In those instances where the manufacturer enforces this policy, it is nice because it levels the playing field with our competitors," Edmunds says. "Because online shoppers are more savvy today and will typically price shop, we find that PoshTots will win the sale more times than not because of our reputation for quality product and excellent customer service."

Follow Edmunds' lead: As you develop the plans for your business, pay careful attention to what your existing competition is doing. Focus on what you can do better and how you can better serve the wants and needs of your target customer base. Also consider what competition is likely to appear in the near future and if you can compete with companies willing and able to spend more money than you on marketing and advertising, or who are able to purchase their inventory in much larger quantities in order to keep their costs down.

Current and Future Demand for Your Products

For your online boutique business to have long-term success potential, you want to offer products that are in demand today and will continue to be in demand in the months and years to come. Through market research, you should be able to determine how quickly your target audience is growing (or shrinking) and whether or not your online business will be viable in six months, one year, three years, five years, and over the long term.

Again, determining the future potential demand for your product requires a strong understanding of the products themselves as well as your target audience, your competition, and any changes that may occur in the marketplace over time. Over time, people's buying habits change, as do their wants and needs. As a business operator, you not only need to understand this concept, but also be able to plan for it and transform your business accordingly to keep up with current and future trends.

Your Passion for the Products

Generally, you're more apt to achieve success with your online boutique if you sell products you truly believe in, you're highly knowledgeable about, and you have a passion for. For example, if you love beautiful clothes and shoes, selling these products to fellow clothing and shoe lovers will be more enjoyable for you than selling products you have little or no interest in. PurePearls.com's Raab believes in this concept wholeheartedly.

"If you want to sell luxury products online successfully, you have to be passionate about it," she says. "Selling luxury products online like PurePearls.com does is not easy because there is an enormous amount of credibility that needs to be gained when doing so. You have to be able to prove to your customers that your products are luxury quality products—sight unseen. Therefore, it takes commitment. I love pearls, so it was not a hard decision for me."

CLICK TIP

One way to find the perfect high-end products to sell is to first focus on what interests you and then consider what types of unique or hard-to-find (non–mass-market) items you personally tend to purchase.

Finding Products to Sell

The next step is to really focus on the products you want to sell and make sure they're viable. Are they among the best products to sell in an online boutique? Should you sell wholesale products or create your own line?

Saladojewelry.com's Valentine suggests doing both. "Start with wholesale, but avoid buying what is available at stores in your area," he says. "Take time to go to the national trade shows in the market you are in. Go every year and find what is not in your area. The goal is to have your buyer, whether online or in the store say that 'you have such unique things.' When word gets out, you take off."

Later, he says, consider your own line. "We are creating a line of jewelry that is made for us and complements our other lines," Valentin says. "So we will sell it as an add-on to existing sales. Otherwise it is way too expensive."

ShopAdorabella.com's Spiegelhalter agrees that both unique items and branded items work best. She recommends carrying unique items—and says developing your own line gives you the ability to set yourself apart. But she has learned that if you do not carry at least a few brands that the majority of people recognize, you aren't going to get visitors searching for brands to your site, and visitors make a site come up in a search engine.

"If you have at least a few brands that people know, it will bring them to your site," she says. "People have to have some way to know about the products you are selling—and also find your website—or else you'll sink."

As you search for high-end items to sell, take advantage of the following resources to find the best opportunities and products that offer the greatest profit potential.

Drop-Shipper Directories

A drop-shipper is a distributor that offers a large selection of high-end products. It sells the products to its dealers at wholesale prices. However, the drop-shipper directly ships all items to your customers (on your behalf), so you never have to acquire any inventory. Your job is simply to market the items and take the order. Before deciding to work with a drop-shipper, you'll want to make sure it's reputable, reliable, and offering quality products.

To find a listing of drop-shippers, using any internet search engine such as Google or Yahoo! and enter the search term "dropshippers" or "drop shippers." Keep in mind that for many luxury products, there are specialist drop-shippers. For example, GoToBaby.com, can drop-ship unique baby products directly to your customers in your business name and even include a gift card that is filled out with your customer's message (if desired). All orders are shipped quickly via UPS and DHL, and the tracking numbers are e-mailed to you directly for you to pass on to your customers.

Importers/Exporters

Importers and exporters are companies that import products (in large quantities) from overseas manufacturers. These manufacturers often don't have retail distribution lined up for themselves. The importer acts as the middleman between the manufacturer and retailers, and typically offers products that can't be purchased elsewhere. When dealing with many importers, however, you'll be required to place large orders for specific products. Working with importers requires some knowledge about business, foreign markets, currency conversion, and international (freight) shipping. The profit margins, however, are potentially higher than if you deal with a wholesaler or distributor based in America. Kompass (kompass-usa.com) offers an online directory of importers and exporters that is searchable by product name, category, or company name.

Local Businesses and Manufacturers

You may discover the perfect item to sell online by visiting local shops, boutiques, and stores. If an item is selling well at a local retail store, chances are it will also sell online to a potentially worldwide market. Once you do pinpoint a product to sell, you can track down its manufacturer or find a wholesaler/distributor that supplies it.

Trade Shows

Every industry has its own trade shows where product developers, manufacturers, wholesalers, and distributors get together to show off their latest offerings. Attending trade shows can help you find products to sell, plus help you meet with suppliers. To find trade shows scheduled for your area (or anywhere in the world for that matter), check out the *Tradeshow Week* (tradeshow week.com), EventsEye (eventseye.com), or BizTrade (biz-tradeshows.com) websites. You can also contact the local convention centers in your city to see what events each will be hosting in the months ahead or look at the "Calendar" or "Events" section of any industry trade publication.

Wholesale Directories

These are directories of wholesalers and distributors who represent product manufacturers and act as the middleman between manufacturers and the retailers who ultimately sell the products to consumers. There are a variety of directories available that list wholesalers and distributors by industry or product category, which makes tracking them down relatively easy. Using any search engine, enter the search phrase "wholesaler directory" to find referrals that offer the types of products you want to sell.

CLICK TIP

Looking for a jewelry supplier resource? Then check out JewelryDealz.com, a website that lists more than 250 jewelry wholesalers, drop-shippers, manufacturers, and online liquidators of fine jewelry closeouts.

Choosing the Right Wholesale Supplier

Beware! Before choosing a wholesaler to work with, remember that there are many fly-by-night companies out there in this space.

So how can you make sure that the items you are buying are actually wholesale products; that you are not really paying retail prices for your inventory; and that you are doing business with a good company? There are certain things that you should look for, and look out for, when shopping for a wholesale supplier. One of the biggest clues that you are about to be taken for a ride is the fact that they insist that you pay a setup fee to use their services. Legitimate wholesale suppliers do not require you to pay a setup or paperwork fee to purchase products from them.

Another ploy that less-than-reputable wholesale suppliers use is to insist you have a website to sell their goods. You are opening an online boutique, but if the wholesale company attempts to hook you into providing its site at a hefty website development fee along with a monthly fee, you should definitely look for your wholesale gifts elsewhere.

If you must pay a monthly membership to a company site just to purchase items, then you are best served by not doing business with that company. There isn't any reputable wholesale company that requires its customers to pay a membership to purchase products.

Before you can buy any wholesale merchandise, you'll need to know what types of payment terms you will have. As you shop around for wholesale suppliers, you'll find that many of them want you to use a credit card as a preferred payment option.

CLICK TIP

A great way to find wholesale partners is goWholesale (gowholesale.com), which connects wholesale firms (which advertise on the site) with buyers seeking products for resale and related business services. Online boutique owners can search by category. The goWholesale's site helps wholesalers reach highly targeted wholesale buyer audiences in a more effective and efficient manner than other major search engine alternatives.

Once you build up a business relationship—and it will take time for trust to build—you may have the option to get a "net in 30" deal. It means that you must pay the balance you owe the wholesaler within 30 days of your order. This arrangement enables you to sell the wholesale items at a profit and pay off what you owe the supplier without pulling your money out of your pocket first. Do not, however, expect to get this deal when you first start buying from the supplier. It just won't happen.

CLICK TIP

For additional ideas about products to sell online, pick up a copy of *202 Things You Can Buy and Sell for Big Profits!*, *2nd Edition*, published by Entrepreneur Press (entrepreneurpress.com) and available wherever books are sold.

A very important factor you need to take into consideration is the cost of the shipping and handling on any merchandise you order. You don't want to purchase your wholesale gifts, only to find that its shipping and handling is so high that the majority of your profit margins are eaten away.

Keep all of these factors in mind before signing on the dotted line with a new wholesale partner.

Chapter 3

Getting to Know Your Target Audience

*N*ow is the time for you to define your online boutique's target audience and decide how you'll best reach that market. Remember that it's to your benefit to know and understand as much as possible about your target customer.

Your Customers

If you understand your audience, know what they're looking for, and can quickly and succinctly address their needs, wants, and concerns on your website—while at the same time promoting a sense of professionalism and confidence in your business—you're more apt to generate a sale.

How does Social Couture's Cabanes get to know her customer base? "Observe, observe, observe–comb your competitors' sites, catalogs, and magazines; visit all the associated blogs; and discuss, e-mail, and market at every opportunity," she says. "Understanding your customer is constant and evolving and will define your ability to effectively market and convert site visitors into customers."

Cabanes says her target audience is clearly defined as women that are comfortable with purchasing products on the internet and have higher levels of disposal income. According to the Census Bureau, women ages 18 to 55 make up more that 50 percent of all online buyers and account for more than 55 percent of all online sales.

ShopAdorabella.com's Spiegelhalter gets to know her customer base by inviting customers to e-mail her with questions. Another great way she receives feedback is by allowing customers and prospective customers to see her wares at a special holiday shows. "Being a new business, it helps get my name out there as well as lets people see my clothing in person, and allows people to talk to me and tell me what they want to see and what they like," Spiegelhalter says. "It's something I really enjoy doing, and I see myself doing it years down the road. They are fun, and I really like hearing and seeing how people react to the clothing I have picked out."

Selling at festivals, markets, and trade shows in your industry are additional great ways to promote your high-end merchandise, and ultimately lead customers back to your online boutique. In general, people who buy from these markets enjoy the experience of buying unique pieces they might not find elsewhere. And keep in mind that advertising your website on your packaging or on the physical presentation area can create sales long after the event is forgotten.

PoshTots.com's Edmunds says a great way she gets to know her customer base is through her company's design consultants, who work closely with the company's customers daily.

The big questions on your mind should be how will you drive potential customers who fall within your target audience to your website, and then once they're at your website, how will you transform them into paying customers. In reality, the process of capturing a web surfer's attention with your website's content must happen in mere seconds or your visitor will simply surf elsewhere.

Establish Your Niche

Most online boutique operators find it easier to select products to sell that cater to a very small niche market. By doing this, it becomes easier to understand your potential customers, address their wants, needs, and concerns, and specifically cater all of your website's content, along with your marketing materials, to this narrowly defined audience.

A niche market can be any group of people that you define as your target audience. It can be based on a single defining factor, such as a special interest. For example, if you're selling a unique, imported handbag, the single criteria you might use to define your target audience is handbag lovers. You can more narrowly define this audience by focusing on just female handbag lovers, handbag lovers who earn a specific income, handbag lovers who live in a specific geographic region, or handbag loves who only shop for imported handbags.

Linda Hayes' Tonic Home says niche marketing is especially essential when selling luxury, high-end products on the web. "The market is narrow so to speak, so you can be much more cost effective with marketing when reaching your target market," she says, adding that her target audience is anyone looking for chic, modern home design. "We found that we do best in big city markets," she says. "Those who live in New York, Los Angeles, San Francisco, and Miami."

Heather Smith, of Coco's Shoppe (cocosshoppe.com), a site offering women's clothing, accessories, and beauty products that are environmentally friendly, caters to a niche market—and has made an effort to get to know her target customers as well as her products. "We are the first true eco-boutique with really, really hip lines," she says. "As a result, we target women aged 20 to 50 who care about how they look *and* their impact on the environment. They

DO YOU HAVE THE RIGHT STUFF?

Despite the millions of dollars luxury e-tailers spend trying to appeal to affluent online shoppers, a Forrester Research study found that it's not working. Luxury e-tailers, it says, miss their target audience. Their most common mistake made? Assuming affluent shoppers want to be dazzled online by extravagance. Based on this assumption, many luxury e-tailers build websites with bandwidth-intensive interfaces that load slowly. Instead of creating a unique shopping experience, in many cases the sites frustrate shoppers.

According to the Forrester Research study, affluent online shoppers don't want to be dazzled. Instead, they want convenience, confidence, and control when shopping online. They want the convenience of easy product research, purchases, and returns. They want to have confidence in the e-store they buy from and in the brand they buy. And they want control over the shopping experience through easy access to quality customer service and personal information protection.

If you want your e-store to appeal to affluent shoppers, here are a few tips:

➡ *Make shopping simple.* Provide a smart search engine so shoppers can quickly find what they're looking for.

➡ *Make it simple for shoppers to research products.* Provide as much information as you can about each product and link to other helpful resources.

➡ *Simplify the purchase and return processes.*

➡ *Clearly communicate the total cost of the purchase before asking for payment information.*

➡ *Build confidence in your store and brand names.*

➡ *Provide quality customer service.*

➡ *Protect your customers' personal information.* Post a privacy policy on your site to reassure shoppers.

Essentially, affluent online shoppers want the same things every other online shopper wants: good customer service, a site that works well but still looks good, brands that inspire confidence, and a commitment to customer privacy.

are educated and looking for high-quality merchandise, and we make every effort to give them what they want and need."

Sometimes your target audience changes as your business grows. "When I initially began, I said women 24 to 39 were my target audience," says ShopAdorabella's Spiegelhalter. "I have found, however, that many younger women and girls like my clothing and accessories, and I have had many women considerably older than my age range buy my merchandise."

Doing Your Market Research

Market research is an important part of the process of defining your audience, and as a result, you should approach your market research from several angles. The internet will be invaluable here. You can use the internet to research some competitors and the high-end products you are planning to sell.

First, focus on the high-end or luxury product you'll be selling and learn as much as you can about the people to whom it will appeal. Take a close look at whatever information is available from the manufacturer or distributors of the product you're planning to sell as well as whatever materials and information is available from your competition. Research what your competition is doing to market the same or similar products. What approach is it taking? Who is its target audience? What primary marketing message is your competition using to sell the product? Based on your knowledge of the product and your target audience, how can you improve or build on what your competition is doing in order to attract your own customers?

Next, do as much research about your target audience as possible. Create a profile. Based on this profile of people you believe will be your primary audience, learn as much as possible about their likes and dislikes, their wants, their needs, and what problems they're facing in their daily lives.

Then focus on how you can use this knowledge and understanding to generate as much interest in your product as possible. How much effort will you have to put into educating your target customer about the product you'll be selling? What information will you need to convey? What is the best way to convey this information in a succinct, easy-to-understand, and cost-effective way that will capture your target audience's attention?

Addressing the Wants and Needs of Your Customers

No matter what you're selling, every consumer buys products based on a need or desire. As someone about to begin selling one or more products online, it's important to understand that the need your customer has for your product can be real or it can be perceived. In other words, the consumer might really and truly need the product, or with the help of your marketing, they can become convinced that they need it in order to solve a problem, make their life somehow easier, or add happiness to their life on some level. This is a perceived need, and it can be just as powerful as a real need in terms of influencing buying habits. As you sell your product, your goal is to make the consumer think, "I need this now!" and get them to ask themselves, "How did I ever live without it?"

In addition to needs, people also have wants and desires. Most people also have some discretionary income they can use to make purchases that can satisfy these various wants and desires. All marketing and advertising is designed to appeal either to a consumer's wants or needs (or both). Luckily, because you are selling high-end products, you can assume your audience has some discretionary income—and therefore can have his needs and wants meet with relative ease.

If a want or need doesn't actually exist for a product you're selling, it becomes your job to create a perceived want or need in the customer's mind. This can be tricky. Executives at advertising agencies, marketing firms, and

---

CLICK TIP

Once you define your target audience, put yourself in its shoes and start to think as it thinks. One way to do this is to read the newspapers, magazines, books and special interest publications they typically read. This should be considered ongoing research because it will help keep you in the know about current trends, issues, concerns, new developments, and information that's of interest to your target audience. It's also information you can use to help you better create a want or need for the product you'll be selling.

---

public relations firms spend years fine-tuning their skills and mastering techniques for influencing peoples' buying habits. Assuming you don't have the budget to hire an advertising agency or public relations firm to help you market and sell your products, these are skills you'll have to learn yourself.

The approach you take, however, must be customized for the product you'll be selling and for the audience you're intending to sell your products to. A certain website design, for example, may work extremely well for selling one product to a specific target audience, but it might not work at all for another product designed to reach a different audience altogether.

Reaching Your Customers

During your online boutique's design phase, it's important that every element and piece of content incorporated into your site be created to cater to your target audience. Just because you have the ability to add flashy bells and whistles to your site (using graphic animations, sound effects, and other elements), it does not mean that you should use them. Use them only if they help you quickly and effectively communicate your sales message and create a demand for what you're selling.

A professional-looking website doesn't have to be overly complex in order to achieve its objectives. In fact more often than not from a website design standpoint, simple, straightforward, easy-to-understand, and simple-to-navigate is better and more effective as a sales tool. We'll cover this in future chapters.

Likewise, as you begin to market your products and drive traffic to your website, you'll want to use proven and cost-efficient marketing, advertising, public relations, and promotional methods that you believe your target audience will relate to and more importantly, respond to favorably to—at a relatively low cost.

In fact, as an online boutique operator, one of your goals should be to become an expert at low-cost, grassroots marketing techniques that allow you to reach a niche audience comprised specifically of people who'd be interested in what you're selling.

Chapter 4

Choosing Your Company Name and Registering Your URL

*Y*ou'll have to select a name for your online boutique, and then you'll need to register your website's URL (website address). The registration process takes just a few minutes and will cost under $10 per URL if you use an internet registrar such as GoDaddy Group Inc. (godaddy.com). Selecting the name could—and should—take much longer.

Brainstorming the Perfect Web Address

The first step in choosing a great name for your online boutique site is brainstorming. Ideally, the address you select you be easy to remember, easy to spell, and obvious to potential web surfers. For example, if the name of your company is "ABC International," you might want your website address to be "ABCInternational.com."

Obviously, with so many websites already in existence, many website domain names are already taken. However, with more than 31.7 trillion potential domain names ending with the ".com" extension, there are still plenty available.

You can have many different URLs for your online boutique, all of which lead to the same place. So, you could potentially register abcinternational.com, abcinternational.biz, and abcinternational.info to ensure web surfers will be able to find you.

If you have your mind set on a name that is already taken in cyberspace, using the generic top-level domains (such as .com, .org, .net, .gov, .biz, or .info), you can use internet country code top-level domains from other countries. For example, instead of buyflowers.com, you can register buyflowers.tv, buyflowers.cc, and buyflowers.ws. These domain names include internet country code top-level domains from, respectively, the Polynesian island nation of Tuvalu, the Territory of Cocos (Keeling) Islands, and Samoa. These domain names have been marketed as alternatives to the more crowded generic top-level domains, where the selection of unregistered domain names is much more limited. The .ws domain name, for example, has achieved some

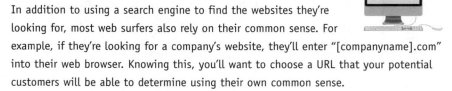

CLICK TIP

In addition to using a search engine to find the websites they're looking for, most web surfers also rely on their common sense. For example, if they're looking for a company's website, they'll enter "[companyname].com" into their web browser. Knowing this, you'll want to choose a URL that your potential customers will be able to determine using their own common sense.

popularity because in this context it stands for "website" or "world site" rather than the abbreviation for Western Samoa, the nation's official name when two-letter country codes were standardized in the 1970s.

Most web surfers are accustomed to URLs ending with the popular .com extension. Ideally, you want your URL to use it. Potential customers might get confused trying to find your website if it utilizes a less popular extension.

The customizable part of a domain name and the extension (.com, for example) can be up to 63 characters long. As a general rule, the shorter the domain name, the easier it is to remember and type into a web browser accurately. Virtually all of the one-, two-, three- and four-character long domain names have long since been taken. Most importantly, the customizable part of the domain name you select must be totally unique and not be registered by another person or company. It also can not violate someone else's copyrighted name, company name, or product name.

Domain names are not case sensitive, so you can mix and match upper- and lower-case letters to make a domain name easier to read and promote. For example, you could promote your domain name as "abccompany.com" or "ABCCompany.com" or "AbcCompany.com."

As you brainstorm the perfect domain name for your business, come up with a list of at least five to ten options you like. When you're ready to register your domain name, you'll first need to determine if the domain name you've selected has already been registered by someone else. This process takes under one minute.

To check if a domain name is registered to someone else, simply go to the website of any domain name registrar, such as GoDaddy Inc. (godaddy.com),

CLICK TIP

As you brainstorm the perfect URL, the part of the website address that you create can only use letters, numbers, and the hyphen symbol (-). No other special characters or punctuation marks (such as !, #, $, or ,) can be used. Also, no spaces can be used within a URL. You can use an underscore (_) to represent a space, but this can be confusing to web surfers. It's not advisable.

Network Solutions Inc. (networksolutions.com), or Register.com Inc. (register.com), and enter your desired domain name in the field marked "Start a domain search" or "Find a domain name." If the domain name you've entered is available, for an annual fee, you will have the opportunity to register it on the spot. If, however, it is already taken, you have three options:

1. You can choose and register an alternative domain name, one that nobody else has.
2. You can contact the person or company that owns the domain name and offer to purchase or lease it. This will typically cost much more than registering a domain name that isn't already taken. Acquiring a domain name from someone else or another company can cost

DOS AND DON'TS FOR DOMAIN NAMES

Here are some rules of thumb to help you select the best domain names:

➡ Short names are best because they reduce the chances for misspellings or for a potential visitor to forget the correct name.

➡ Avoid plurals, hyphens, and abbreviations unless they are part of your brand name or the correct spelling of a word.

➡ The domain name should be easy to communicate verbally. For example, the name should slip off your tongue when you meet people on the street. It should also be memorable so they will remember it when they get home without writing it down.

➡ A domain name should include your brand name and/or keywords that make your product easier for customers to find. Rather than a nondescriptive name like jonesbrothers.com, a better choice might be jonesbrotherssaddles.com.

➡ A dotcom (.com) domain is usually the best choice rather than .net , .org, etc. Customers usually try typing a name ending in .com first and may become sidetracked and go elsewhere if you are not there.

DOS AND DON'TS FOR DOMAIN NAMES, CONTINUED

➡ Names high in the alphabet help if directories or other services list domains in alphabetical order.

➡ Be sure the name you choose is not someone else's registered trade name or trademark. You can look up the name with the United States Patent and Trademark Office (uspto.gov/) and your state's trademark database.

➡ When you find your best choice for a domain, register it immediately because someone else may register it if you delay.

➡ Eliminate prefixes. Once on the web server, your web master can set up your site so that when you type in the web address, you do not have to type in the prefixes of "www." and "http://" That will give you an advantage because folks can find you both ways (www.yourdomain.com or http://www.yourdomain.com). Those who do not type in those prefixes can also find the site and not receive a "site not found" message.

---

anywhere from under $100 to $1,000,000, depending on the domain name.

3. You can register to be put on a waiting list and be notified when and if the domain name you want ever becomes available. The chances of this happening, however, are relatively slim.

After you've determined that the domain name you want is available, you'll need to register it with an internet Domain Name Registrar. There is an annual fee to register a domain name. Depending on the registrar, registering a single domain name will cost between $5.95 and $39.95. Obviously, choose a company with the lowest rates. GoDaddy.com tends to offer very competitive rates for domain name registrations, plus this company makes the process extremely fast and easy.

Registering your domain name requires you to provide details about yourself and your company, including your name, address, phone number, and

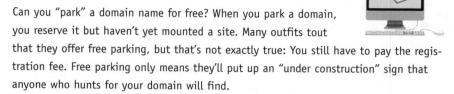

CLICK TIP

Can you "park" a domain name for free? When you park a domain, you reserve it but haven't yet mounted a site. Many outfits tout that they offer free parking, but that's not exactly true: You still have to pay the registration fee. Free parking only means they'll put up an "under construction" sign that anyone who hunts for your domain will find.

credit card information (for paying the annual fee). The process will vary based on which domain registrar you use, but it should take no more than five to ten minutes to complete. After you've set up an account, registering additional domain names can be done much faster.

Part of the domain name registration process will most likely involve providing the registrar with your internet aervice provider's IP address. You may also need to provide what are called DNS numbers to the registrar. This is information that will be provided by your internet service provider (ISP), if applicable. The ISP is the company that will be hosting your website. In this case, it'll probably be the company you select to provide you with an e-commerce turnkey solution.

Ideally, you want your website to have a single domain name that you can promote and will be easy to remember. However, because some people have trouble spelling or get easily confused, you might want to register multiple domain names with slightly different spellings. That way, if someone accidentally types the wrong domain name into their web browser, they'll still wind up at your website. Think about some of the common typos or ways someone might misspell your domain name, and register those domain names as well.

Also, to ensure you generate the most traffic possible to your website, consider registering domain names that relate to the products you'll be selling. Think about the search phrases or terms someone who is looking for your products online might use, and incorporate those terms into your domain name. So if someone is looking for a widget and they type "widget.com" into their browser, they'll find your website. Be creative as you register your domain names, keeping in mind that it's perfectly OK to have ten or more domain names ending up at the same website.

CATCHING DROP CATCHERS

Some e-tailers today who accidentally let their domain names expire are becoming victims of drop catchers—people who try to catch web names that others let expire. Currently, there are hundreds of drop catchers that buy the names and resell them or use them for websites loaded with advertisements.

"This has been going on since 1997, but over the past few years it has been growing as the number of registries has been increasing," says Jay Westerdal, CEO, Name Intelligence Inc., a Bellevue, Washington-based company that that tracks the industry. Industry experts say that roughly 200,000 expired domain names become available everyday. But while many are consciously discarded by their owners, others are mistakes.

So how do you protect yourself and make sure you do not become a victim? For starters, follow these tips from Warren Adelman, president/COO of Scottsdale, Arizona-based GoDaddy.com, the largest domain registrar in the world with 12.9 million domains under management. The company sells domains to customers, but it also runs a domain name auction, which allows people who own names to put those names into the auction for sale, and in that auction it also sells expired names.

➡ *Make sure your contact information is up to date.* Why? Because renewal notices go to that contact information. "If you register a name for 12 months, at a certain point before the end of that year, we or other registries are going to communicate with you and let you know (via e-mail or direct mail) that your domain is going to expire in 90, 60, 30, 15, 7, 2 days, or 1 day," says Adelman. "So make sure your contact information, including your e-mail address and your physical mailing address is up to date." Adelman also says that typically registrars give users a grace period after their registration expires—at GoDaddy.com it is 30 days. Within that time, the registrar can still come back renew to their names. And, even if a name totally expires and goes into an auction, "we don't reassign it until 30 days goes by. So that still gives a customer the opportunity to come back and say, 'Hey, I really meant to renew it.' "

CATCHING DROP CATCHERS, CONTINUED

➡ *Don't use a free e-mail account.* Adelman also suggests not using a free e-mail account for your contact information when registering for a domain name. "Oftentimes people will do this, and it's not an e-mail contact they necessarily use all the time, and oftentimes, with a free e-mail account, if you don't access them in 30 days, they go away," he says.

➡ *Take advantage of auto renew.* Most registries offer this service, which allows consumers or businesses who buy a domain name for a year to auto renew at the end of that year for an extra year by charging the credit card that they gave the registry. "If you do that, you won't have any chance of losing [your domain name]," says Adelman, who adds that you should also make sure you keep your payment information up to date. Adelman also suggests registering your domain name for more than one year, especially because in most cases, your costs go down if you register your domain name for multiple years.

Chapter 5

Tools You'll Need to Get Started

*B*y now you realize that a lot goes into finding the perfect luxury products to sell in your online boutique and then pinpointing the perfect target market for that product. Once these important steps are completed, you're ready to establish your online boutique's business's infrastructure and develop the website you'll use to market and sell your products.

So it is time to outline the tools you'll need to move forward, tools to establish your business and then to get it online and fully operational. By defining your needs early in the process, you'll more easily be able to create a preliminary budget.

The tools we will be discussing here include computers, software, computer peripherals, internet access, to name a few.

Keep in mind that the steps for establishing the infrastructure for your business that are outlined in this chapter will take most people more than one day to complete. Plan on spending up to several weeks laying the groundwork for your business and creating its infrastructure. Part of this process involves determining how your business will operate on a day-to-day basis, what tools and services will be used, and what methods you'll use to handle important tasks, such as credit card payment and order processing. Because every business's needs are totally different, it's important to properly research and understand your options and then choose solutions that best fit your needs and budget.

Gathering the Equipment You'll Need

Because you're going to be launching an online boutique to tap the millions of web surfers out there, for this venture you'll need, of course, a PC or Mac computer with access to the internet. Depending on your lifestyle and budget, you may opt to purchase a desktop computer and set up a formal office in your home. There are many great deals to be had on state-of-the-art desktop computers from local computer retailers and office supply superstores, as well as online.

For a new PC-based desktop computer, plan on spending under $1,000, but more if you also need peripherals and software. Mac desktop computers from Apple (apple.com) tend to cost a bit more.

Laptop computers, which are convenient if you plan to do a lot of traveling for your online boutique, cost more than otherwise comparable desktop computers. But they can be invaluable. Using a laptop computer gives you added mobility and allows you to manage your business from virtually anywhere (as long as access to the internet is available). For a new PC laptop computer that runs Microsoft's Windows Vista (microsoft.com), for example, you'll probably spend $600 to $1,500. A MacBook from Apple is priced starting at $1,100.

In addition to the computer itself, you'll need to load your computer or laptop with business software. If you don't already have the core suite of applications you'll need, plan on spending between $500 and $2,500 for software.

Microsoft Office (microsoft.com) offers word processing, spreadsheet management, and a range of other applications. You might also want to invest in some accounting or bookkeeping software, such as QuickBooks by Intuit Software (quickbooks.intuit.com), or Microsoft Money (microsoft.com), to help manage your business's finances. The finance software you use should be able to print invoices and packing slips for your customers.

Special software to help you manage a database of your customers, suppliers, and other important business contacts is also extremely useful. Microsoft Outlook, part of Microsoft Office (microsoft.com), Act! from Sage Software (act.com), or the Address Book software that comes bundled with Mac computers can be used for this purpose.

Based on what you'll be selling, you might need to take and edit your own product photos to incorporate into your website. For this, you'll need software such as PhotoShop CS3 or Photoshop Elements (a scaled-down version of PhotoShop) from Adobe (adobe.com). Again, depending on the tools you use to develop and maintain your website, you may need to acquire off-the-shelf website design and publishing software. Adobe offers products that are considered the industry standard for website design, creation, and publishing.

Another part of your computer investment will be in peripherals, such as a printer, speakers, a scanner, and a data backup device (such as an external hard drive). Prices vary dramatically for these items. To save money and desk space, consider investing in an all-in-one printer, scanner, fax machine, and photocopier. For the type of all-in-one machine you'll need, plan on spending from $150 to $300.

When it comes to internet access, you have a variety of options. You can acquire extremely inexpensive dial-up access to the web for under $20 per month. This provides a slow connection and makes it virtually impossible to utilize many of the internet's multimedia capabilities. Because you'll be running

DSL VS. BROADBAND

DSL service provides always-on, high-speed internet access over a single dedicated telephone line. This technology allows voice and data communications to use the same line simultaneously. So you can use the internet without interfering with your ability to send or receive telephone calls.

The predominant DSL service in commercial use for business and residential customers is ADSL (asymmetrical DSL). It offers differing upload and download speeds and can be configured to deliver speeds from the network to the customer up to 120 times faster than dialup service. Typically, the delivered download speed for most networks is in the range of 50 times faster than ordinary 28.8 kbps dial-up. The slower upload speed, while not as fast as cable, is more than adequate for sending files and documents to other people or pages to a website.

Cable broadband service also offers an always-on high speed internet connection, but over a cable television. While cable modems may have greater downloading capabilities than dialup, that bandwidth is "shared" among users on the system. Connection speed will, therefore, vary, sometimes dramatically, when more users are online at the same time.

Although many cable systems have the capability to deliver from 10 to 20 Mbps (megabits per second) of download speed, most limit system downloads. Typical download speeds for most residential cable services are in the 3 Mbps range. Many cable systems now offer a "value internet service" with 1.5 Mbps download speed to compete with lower-priced DSL service, but they do not always advertise it. You have to ask.

Too many people trying to send or receive data on a cable network at the same time causes congestion and slows the cable connection speed (upload and download) considerably. In many instances, this congestion causes cable to be slower than DSL.

an online business, you'll be better served by obtaining high-speed DSL or broadband internet access through your local cable television provider, phone company, or internet service provider.

For a high-speed internet connection, plan on spending between $29.95 and $49.95 per month for unlimited web access. In addition to this fee, you'll still need to pay a monthly fee for a turnkey website design and e-commerce solution in order to design, create, and manage your website.

Other Equipment

As you set up your office, other tools and equipment you'll probably find useful include:

- Briefcase
- Credit card payment processing equipment and software
- Desk and desk chair
- Filing cabinets
- Floor and desk lamp(s)
- Office supplies
- Postage machine and postage scale
- Printer stand
- Shipping supplies
- Telephone
- Telephone service (including long distance, caller ID, call waiting, voice mail, etc.)
- Wastepaper basket

Should you obtain an incoming toll-free phone number for your business? Absolutely! This type of number allows you to easily stay in touch with both your customers and your prospective customers. What's more, it gives your business added

CLICK TIP

Once your business grows and becomes successful, you might opt to hire an outside company to accept, handle, and process all of your incoming telephone orders, as well as your order fulfillment from your internet-based orders. This will free up your time, but will reduce your profits, because you'll need to pay for these services.

CLICK TIP

If you'll be storing a lot of inventory, seriously consider purchasing separate business insurance that will cover you against loss, theft, or damage. The inventory for your business probably won't be covered by your homeowner's or renter's insurance policy.

credibility; you must be a reputable company if you can afford this service. They also give you an edge over competition, giving customers the feeling that you care about their convenience.

You might also want to rent a box from your local post office. Why? Because if you rent a box and use that address on your promotional mail and stationery, you will make it less obvious that you are working from home (if you are). The professional image you portray is very important to your clientele. It's also cheap; just $26-$38 per year.

Your local office supply superstore such as OfficeMax (officemax.com), Staples (staples.com), or Office Depot (officedepot.com) is a good place to shop for office furniture, equipment and supplies. Still, you're apt to find lower prices if you shop online. The NexTag.com (nextag.com) price comparison website, for example, is a great place to find what you're looking for at the lowest price possible–whether it's specific computer or consumer electronics equipment, business tools, or office supplies (such as ink or toner for your printer).

During the office setup process, consider where and how you'll store your inventory until it's sold. You must be able to safely store your inventory until it's ready to ship, yet at the same time, you want your inventory to be easily accessible. Chances are, you'll need to find a climate-controlled, dry environment, which typically rules out most attics and basements. Having to run back and forth to an off-site storage facility will be inconvenient, but may be necessary if you can't store your inventory in your home or apartment.

A Well-Thought-Out Site

What makes a good website—luxury or otherwise? Before getting enmeshed in design details, get the big picture by writing a site outline. A well-thought-out site outline includes: Content, structure, design, navigation, and credibility. Keep these concepts in mind as you begin to plot out your site. Of course, you'll most likely be using an e-commerce turnkey solution to design, create, publish, and manage your website, so you won't be doing any programming.

A web page is a text document that usually includes formatting and links to other pages. This special formatting is composed of tags, which are part of hypertext markup language (HTML) and are used to link one page, section, or image to another.

For your online boutique, you'll probably select a template from one of these turnkey solutions to use during the design process. The ISP provides your e-commerce turnkey solution will probably have dozens, if not hundreds, of website design templates from which to choose.

CLICK TIP

Don't go crazy with color. This is one of the biggest goofs of new web page designers. Stick with maybe two colors for fonts (words), and use a simple, basic color for the page background (white, off-white, and pale yellow are good choices). Always test your page on a laptop with a very cheap screen— don't assume surfers will have high-end monitors. If it doesn't look good on a small, cheap screen, it's bad page design.

After choosing a template that offers the overall design and color scheme you believe best represents your company and its products in cyberspace, you'll need to customize the template and create your site. For easy implementation into your website, you'll want to have all photos, graphics, and illustrations in a .JPG or .TIF graphic format (having at least 300 dpi resolution).

CLICK TIP

Beware of copyright and trademark infringement! Make sure you have written permission to use any text, photos, graphics, illustrations, or other copyrighted or trademarked materials you plan to use on your website. This applies to any material (text, graphics, audio, photographs, videos, animations, logos, etc.) that you did not create yourself from scratch and that you do not own the rights to. If you'll be using product artwork or product descriptions created by the manufacturer or the product you'll be selling, for example, make sure you have permission to use these materials before incorporating them into your online boutique.

THE TEN MOST DEADLY MISTAKES IN SITE DESIGN

Avoid these gaffes, and your site will be far better than much of the competition.

1. *Disabling the "back" button*. Evil site authors long ago figured out how to break a browser's back button so that when a user pushes it, undesired things happen: There's an immediate redirect to an unwanted location, the browser stays put because the back button has been deactivated, or a new window pops up and overtakes the screen. Porno site authors are masters of this—their codes are often so malicious that frequently the only way to break the cycle is to restart the computer. This trick has gained currency with other site builders. My advice: Never do it. All that's accomplished is that viewers get annoyed.

2. *Opening new windows*. Once upon a time, using multiple new frames to display content as a user clicked through a site was cool—a new thing in web design. Now it only annoys viewers because it ties up system resources, slows computer response, and generally complicates a surfer's experience. Sure, it's easy to use this tool. But don't.

3. *Failing to put a phone number and address in a plainly seen location*. If you're selling, you need to offer viewers multiple ways to contact you. The smartest route is to put up a "Contact Us" button that leads to complete information—mailing address, phone, and fax number. Even if nobody ever calls, the very presence of this information comforts some viewers.

4. *Broken links*. Bad links—hyperlinks that do nothing when clicked—are the bane of any surfer. Test your site—and do it weekly—to ensure that all links work as promised.

5. *Slow server times*. Slow times are inexcusable with professional sites. It's an invitation to the visitor to click away. What's slow? There is no easy rule, but any click should lead to something immediately happening. Maybe a new page or image takes a few seconds to come into view, but the process should at least start immediately.

THE TEN MOST DEADLY MISTAKES, CONTINUED

6. *Outdated information.* Again, there's no excuse, but it's stunning how many site builders lazily leave up pages that long ago ceased to be accurate. When information changes, update the appropriate pages immediately—and this means every bit of information, every fact, even tiny ones. As a small business, you cannot afford the loss of credibility that can come from having even a single factual goof.

7. *Scrolling text and marquees.* It's an odd fact, but Netscape and Microsoft Internet Explorer do not display pages identically, which is one way these site-design tools get easily screwed up by browsers. Scrolling can also be maddening to the viewer who wants to know—now—what you're offering, but the information keeps scrolling off the page. Use these tools in personal pages—they are fun and add liveliness to otherwise static pages—but put these tricks aside when building business pages.

8. *Too many font styles and colors.* Pages ought to present a unified, consistent look, but novice site builders—entranced by having hundreds of fonts at their fingertips and dozens of colors—frequently turn their pages into a garish mish-mash. Use two or three fonts and colors per page, maximum. The idea is to reassure viewers of your solidity and stability, not to convince them you are wildly artistic.

9. *Orphan pages.* Memorize this: Every page in your site needs a readily seen link back to the home page. Why? Sometimes users will forward a URL to friends, who may visit and may want more information. But if the page they get is a dead end, forget it. Always put a link to Home on every page to solve this problem.

10. *Using leading-edge technology.* Isn't that what the web is all about, especially when the number of Americans who have broadband at home increases every-day? Nope. Your pages need to be readable with a standard, plain-Jane browser, preferably last year's or earlier. State-of-the-art is cool for techno wizards but death for entrepreneurs.

CLICK TIP

Check your site for broken links, automatically and for free, with a stop at Keynote NetMechanic (netmechanic.com). Type in your URL, and—whoosh!—you will get a report on broken links and page load time, and even a freebie spell check. It can also give a free report on browser compatibility on the spot.

Creating Your Site's Text

If you believe you can write copy for your online boutique that will capture the attention of your visitors, effectively communicate your marketing message, and help you sell your products online, then by all means write your own website copy for the product descriptions and other text-based elements on your site.

Your text must be error free in terms of spelling, punctuation, and grammar mistakes. Because you are selling luxury items, it should also have an air of sophistication about it. Stay away from inside jokes or terms such as mark down or clearance.

However, because your potential customers will rely on the text-based elements on your website, such as your product descriptions, to ultimately

A STREAMLINED APPROACH

SimplySoles.com, in Washington, D.C., is one e-tailer finding success in the online luxury market. The company, which sells the best in women's footwear through its catalog and website, brings in an average of $325 on each sale. Sales surpassed $1 million last year.

A key to the site's success is its stream-lined approach. It features only a few designers and a few styles per designer, and the shoes and information are presented in a creative way. "By offering a streamlined collection of truly unique items, there is more [of a] chance that something will catch the eye and speak to visitors on an emotional level," says Kassie Rempel, owner and founder of SimplySoles. "When you are dealing with a $400 pair of shoes, your visitors don't want to have to sort through 10 pages of really small images."

make their buying decision, you might seriously consider hiring a professional freelance writer or marketing expert to create these text-based elements on your behalf.

CLICK TIP

Need to hire an experienced writer, programmer, website designer, photographer, or graphic artist? The eLance.com (elance.com) website allows you to post your needs and have freelance professionals provide you with bids to do the work.

A freelance writer, advertising specialist, public relations professional, or marketing expert will have the skills and experience necessary to create well-written copy for your site. Plan on spending at least several hundred dollars to have a professional writer create product descriptions and other text-based elements for your site. An experienced writer will typically charge between $.50 and $1 per word, or quote a flat fee for a specific project. However, it's not a good idea to negotiate an hourly rate for a writer.

The Kind of Text to Post

In addition to detailed product descriptions, a well-designed and professional online boutique site will have other text-based elements that educate the customer and convey your marketing massage. Additional text-based elements you might want to add to your online boutique include:

- Company description and background information ("About Us")
- Press releases
- FAQ ("Frequently Asked Questions") documents
- Shipping information
- Product return information
- Customer satisfaction guarantee and customer testimonials
- Contact information
- Website copyright information

Education is very important to online boutique owners. Because customers are buying high-ticket items, they want to know as much as possible about the products you are selling before finalizing their order.

Education is extremely important to WhiteFlash.com, a Houston e-tailer that sells diamonds. The company offers a comprehensive diamond library with commentary from gemologists, appraisers, former diamond graders, and professional educators. Visitors can educate themselves about diamonds in the site's "About Diamonds" section. Unique videos help visitors understand and clearly see the diamonds. "Our most informed customer is our best customer," says Debi Wexler, CEO and co-founder. "Our clients gain the confidence to buy when they can leisurely view diamonds and our video tutorials. With confidence comes trust and repeat business." Wexler says the company spends about 5 percent of its $10 million in sales on educational materials for customers.

Creating Professional-Quality Product Photos

One thing is for sure: How well you depict your products online, in terms of the quality of photographs you incorporate into your site, will play a tremendous role in building your credibility and generating sales, especially when selling high-end, luxury goods. With high-end products, your text-based product descriptions are important, but it's essential that you showcase your products visually using multiple, visually appealing photographs.

If you are on a tight budget, you may decide to use vendor- or manufacturer-supplied photographs of merchandise if they have already created a selection of quality product images you can incorporate into your site. These images could be sent from the manufacturer on a disk, or they could e-mail you photographs in a high-resolution format.

Another alternative is to contact a few stock photo agencies to see if you can acquire inexpensive, royalty-free images of your products for your website. To use these images, you either pay a fee per image you use or pay a flat fee for use of an unlimited number of images from the agency's library. A typical stock photo agency will have a library consisting of hundreds of thousands or even millions of digital images available.

The following are a few stock photo agencies worth contacting to obtain stock photographs for your website:

➡ office.microsoft.com/en-us/clipart/default.aspx

➡ adobe.com/products/creativesuite/stockphotos/

➡ bigstockphoto.com

➡ Comstock.com

➡ FotoSearch.com

➡ iStockPhoto.com

➡ Shutterstock.com

Many owners of online boutiques decide to use freelance photographers to take their pictures. But this could backfire, according to ShopAdorabella's Spiegelhalter. "In the beginning I hired a very expensive, fabulous photographer to take my pictures," she says. "The pictures came out beautiful, I couldn't have asked for more, even though bill that was almost $3000. That was a rookie mistake. I quickly learned after that that I would never make a profit if I did that."

What did Spiegelhalter do? She bought a really nice camera and backdrop, and hired several different photographers to come in and teach her lighting and Photoshop. "It took a long time," she says. "Early pictures on my website are definitely lacking to say the least. However, after months and months of practicing and learning, I think I am close to getting it down pat. I am still not a professional photographer, but I think the clothes and accessories look true to form."

Many online boutique owners do take their own product images using a high-resolution digital camera and a photo studio set up in their home, for example. If the products you'll be photographing are small, you can set up an inexpensive desktop photo studio for a few hundred dollars (plus the price of a camera). For larger products, you'll need to use professional-quality lighting and backgrounds to create professional images.

For professional and amateur photographers alike, the Canon EOS Digital Rebel line of cameras (usa.canon.com/consumer) is ideal for taking product photos for the

CLICK TIP

When taking product photographs, you should use a solid color background. Depending on the product and how the photos will be used on your site, a solid white background typically works best. However, using photo editing software like PhotoShop CS3, you can crop away the background altogether, if desired.

OUTSOURCING PHOTOGRAPHY

If you want some professional digital photography on your site, check out eFashionStudio, from eFashionSolutions (efashionsolutions.com), a leading e-commerce provider for the branded fashion apparel/accessories, entertainment and specialty retail industries. The service is a photography-only offering.

From its 6,500 square foot design studio, eFashionStudio helps brands and retailers enhance their online presence through superior digital photography—still and live model shoots—and video fashion shows, and 360-degree product views. It is staffed with professional photographers, editors, color retouchers and correctors, hair and make-up stylists and trainers for live model shoots to deliver the high-quality images the fashion industry demands and the superior image optimization eCommerce requires. Enhanced visual display of product has been proven to increase conversion rates and sales while decreasing returns. Without interrupting warehousing and shipping programs or switching e-commerce platforms, brands can use eFashionStudio services to increase online revenues and profits.

For more information, check out efashionstudio.com.

web. The Digital Rebel XTi, for example, offers 10.1 megapixel resolution and three-frames-per-second shooting with virtually no delay. Add a proper background and appropriate lighting, and with a bit of practice, just about anyone can take professional-quality product photographs worthy of being used on an e-commerce website.

For several hundred dollars, you can purchase the lighting and backgrounds needed to take professional-quality product shots. Lighting and background packages can be purchased from companies like Photography Lighting Company (photography-lighting.com) and Amvona (amvona.com). Another great place to find used or close-out professional photography equipment that's on sale is eBay (ebay.com).

Once you've taken your product photos, you can edit and manipulate them as needed using software such as Adobe Photoshop Elements, Adobe

Photoshop CS3, Apple's iPhoto, or Apple's Aperture, and then incorporate the images into your website. To learn more about Adobe Photoshop, visit the Adobe website (adobe.com). Because you are selling high-value merchandise, you may want to add rich media features to your graphics and photography: allowing viewers to zoom in or view products from a 360-degree angle (covered later).

Your Company's Logo

As a luxury boutique owner, you'll want to make sure your company offers great style and has a great brand. A good way to do this is to create a single-color or multi-colored graphic image that establishes a visual icon to represent

SITE DESIGN TIPS FOR ONLINE SELLERS OF LUXURY GOODS

eMarketers' Jeffrey Grau offers the following tips for luring luxury shoppers to your website—and keeping them there.

1. *Be descriptive.* "The number-one thing to focus on is education," says Grau. "When people are buying expensive items such as jewelry or cars online, they want to know as much as possible about what they are buying before they actually purchase them."

2. *Focus on top-quality visuals.* "Luxury goods require higher-quality images and special features that allow consumers to zoom in or view something from a 360-degree perspective," Grau says.

3. *Offer stellar customer service.* "Make the luxury shopper's experience a great one," Grau says. "For example, make it easy for them to return something they are not happy with. This helps overcome any reservations they may have about purchasing big-ticket items."

a company. A logo can also make use of a specific or custom-designed font or typestyle to spell out your company's name. Having a visually appealing logo helps your company establish credibility and recognition, plus it helps set your company apart from its competition. Once you have a company logo created, you'll want to showcase it prominently on your website, especially in the masthead area.

A logo can be created on a computer using graphics software, or it can be hand-drawn by an artist or graphic designer. Ultimately, the logo will need to be transformed into a digital image in order to be incorporated into your website.

Because your logo is an essential part of your company's branding and identity, you'll want it to look professional, be memorable, and be visually appealing. Ideally, you should hire a graphic artist to help you design your company logo. You can find professional graphic designers who specialize in freelance logo design using a service like eLance.com. Using any internet search engine, you can also use the search phrase "logo design."

When hiring an artist, make sure they are willing to create a handful of potential logo designs for you. You can then narrow down your choices and have one of the designs fine-tuned by the artist to create what you believe will be the perfect logo to represent your company. Plan on spending anywhere from $100 to several thousand dollars to have your logo professionally created. Off-the-shelf logo design software (designed for amateurs) is available, but the end results are typically less professional than if you were to have a professional graphic designer do the work.

In addition to showcasing your logo on your website, it should also be used on your company letterhead, business cards, and brochures, as well as in your online and print ads, and potentially your product's packaging as well (if applicable).

Chapter 6

E-Commerce Turnkey Solutions

*U*ntil recently, if you wanted to launch an e-commerce website to sell products online, you needed to be a computer guru with a thorough understanding of HTML programming, Java, Flash, and a wide range of other complex programming languages and software-based website design tools.

You also needed to invest weeks, often months, in creating from scratch a website capable of handling the functionally needed to securely sell products online. Of course, a team of programmers and graphic designers could also be hired (at a significant expense) to handle much of the programming for you, but as the website operator, you still needed a good understanding of website design and programming.

These days, however, a handful of well-known, established companies offer complete e-commerce turnkey solutions that allow ordinary people with no programming or graphic design knowledge whatsoever to use a set of tools and professionally designed templates to effortlessly design and publish awesome looking and extremely powerful websites in a matter of hours–not days or months. Best of all, many of these turnkey solutions have a very low startup cost (often under $100).

These solutions also include the tools needed to begin accepting orders and online credit card payments for those orders. In other words, you don't need to set up a costly credit card merchant account with a local bank or financial institution to begin accepting Visa, MasterCard, American Express, or Discover credit card or debit card payments. This alone eliminates a significant barrier to entry. Most also allow customers to pay via PayPal (paypal.com), an online payment system that handles all major credit cards, verifies them automatically in real time, has no startup costs, no monthly fee, and charges you 2.9 percent or less per transaction (more on PayPal on page 83).

In general, these solutions—which are probably offered by your ISP—include a suite of site-building tools, product catalog tools, content management tools, shopping cart technology, payment, shipping, marketing strategies, tracking and reporting capabilities, domain registration, and hosting.

More specifically, a good, basic turnkey e-commerce solution would include: preformatted storefront design templates that can be modified by selecting themes, changing colors and fonts, and changing the page layout within a point-and-click administration panel; a web-based store administration tool that allows uses to work on your online store wherever you have an internet connection; integrated site search and browsing, which gives visitors the ability to search your online store by product and browse by price, category, and brand; and inventory management for all of your products.

The solution should also enable your online boutique to offer visitors product variations such as sizes or colors without having to upload each option individually; different category levels that enable users to search through your catalog easily; and, real-time inventory control.

The solution should also be fully integrated with a variety of payment gateways (more about that on page 83) and accept credit card payments with a payment gateway (although a merchant account is required); integration—with real-time calculations—with the major delivery service companies (UPS, FedEx, and USPS); automated tax rates and calculations; and flat rate and/or free shipping offers.

Nowadays, most solutions also offer search engine marketing and optimization tools; express checkout for registered users; the ability for customers to track and view order history; automated order confirmation e-mails; site reporting; free 24/7 customer service; and high-levels of security.

While most of the solutions offer the same features, before making a final decision on the solution you choose, make sure the e-commerce hosting provider offers some sort of scalability, so that when you do expand—and you do want to expand—you will be able to evolve your online boutique into a custom site without the hassle of having to switch ecommerce hosting providers.

In addition, before choosing a provider, remember that there is no better way to evaluate their services than by speaking with their existing clients. Find out what e-stores—or online boutiques, in this case—are already up and running on the e-commerce hosting servers you're considering. Contact the webmasters via the "Contact Us" page and ask if they're happy with their current e-commerce hosting provider.

Then, whatever their answer, find out why. Ask how often if ever the server is down. Ask about help-desk support. Most webmasters will be more than happy to proffer rave (or reprehensible, when appropriate) reviews of their ecommerce hosting provider. More than any other research method, this will help you choose what e-commerce hosting company may be right for you.

Many online boutique owners also swear by hosted solutions from the bigger names in web hosting: 1&1 internet (1and1.com), GoDaddy Group Inc. (godaddy.com), Hostway Corporation (hostway.com), iPower (ipower.com), Network Solutions Inc. (networksolutions.com), ProStores Inc. (prostores.com), Verio Inc. (verio.com), Web.com Inc. (web.com), and Yahoo! (yahoo.com). Even retail giant Amazon.com is getting into the act; it offers a service called

"Selling on Amazon.com" through its Amazon Business Solutions' offering (amazonservices.com).

The cost for these plans starts at about $30 to $40 per month, plus setup fees ranging from free to $50 per month. Some companies also charge transaction fees. Keep in mind, $40 will get you basic functionality; if you want more, such as promotional merchandising tools and fully-customized site designing, you may have to spend a few hundred dollars per month.

Why Amazon?

Selling on Amazon is a good source because it allows you to sell your products on Amazon.com (amazon.com), a leading website and stop for millions of online shoppers. With over 66 million active customer accounts worldwide, your products are exposed to millions of potential customers every day.

With Selling on Amazon, it's easy to upload your inventory. Once you've registered, use the web-based tools, a free desktop software application, or text files to get up and running fast.

Amazon.com also makes buying your products a snap. With features like 1-Click and a brand millions of consumers trust, customers make quick, easy, worry-free purchases. Amazon notifies you by e-mail when an order has been placed. At that time, you pack and ship your item to your customer-unless you let Fulfillment by Amazon do it. That service enables Amazon.com to pick, pack, and ship all of your merchandise. Amazon then deposits payment into your bank account, and sends you an e-mail message notifying you that your payment has been sent.

Besides Selling on Amazon and Fulfillment by Amazon, other services from Amazon Business Solutions include:

➡ *Product Ads on Amazon.com.* Product Ads is an advertising program that allows sellers to promote their products on amazon.com. As a seller, you simply upload your catalog and set your cost-per-click bids. Amazon will then display highly targeted ads for your items on select product and search pages. Customers can click over to your website and purchase the product directly from you (more on cost-per-click programs in Chapter 7).

FREE HOSTED SOLUTIONS?

Yes, it's true. Microsoft and Google have launched beta versions of free hosted web solutions. In 2006, Microsoft launched a version of its Microsoft Office Live service that provides small businesses with a basic package including their own domain name, website, and e-mail accounts for free. The company charges monthly fees, however, for more ramped up packages. For more information, check out the following website: smallbusiness.officelive.com.

Google has also begun offering a similar free solution called Google Apps for Your Domain. It allows small businesses to design and publish their organization's website (but you bring your own domain name) for free. The service also enables small businesses to offer private-labeled e-mail, instant messaging, and calendar tools to all of their users for free. It's all hosted by Google, so there's no hardware or software to install or maintain. Companies must submit a request to be a part of the beta. For more information, check out google.com/a/help/intl/en/index.html.

➡ *WebStore by Amazon.* Use Amazon's world-class e-commerce and merchandising technology to create your own online store and take advantage of benefits such as one place for all your online needs, one toolset to manage WebStore by Amazon, Selling on Amazon, and Fulfillment by Amazon and one interface for managing your inventory, product information, and orders.

➡ *Drop Ship by Amazon.* Here you can use one supplier (Amazon) to sell millions of products to your customers, while maintaining no inventory and no warehouse. You place orders for Amazon products using Drop Ship by Amazon, and Amazon will ship them directly to your customers. Take advantage of its broad and deep product selection and provide your customers with the products they need at extremely competitive prices. It carries a full array of products in categories that include electronics, books, DVDs, computers, home and garden, clothing and jewelry, sports and fitness, and more.

Yahoo! Merchant Solutions

In terms of the e-commerce solutions listed on page 69, Yahoo! Small Business's Yahoo! Merchant Solutions (smallbusiness.yahoo.com/ecommerce) is perhaps the leading place online boutique owners turn to for help setting up their e-commerce stores. Currently, more than 40,000 online merchants, about one out of every eight online stores, uses the Yahoo! e-commerce platform.

Jacquelyn Tran, president and founder of Perfume Bay Inc., a Huntington Beach, California-based company that sells high-end cosmetics, perfume, skin-care products, and home fragrances and candles on its website Perfumebay.com, uses a full-featured e-commerce service from Yahoo!.

Tran started Perfume Bay in 1999, and now offers more than 700 unique brands of perfume and thousands of other fragrance and beauty products from her Huntington Beach store and e-commerce site. Yet during startup, Tran knew nothing about the internet and hired a web designer to build her site. The customized site was expensive, however; it cost her $50,000. "This included advertising, a custom-built shopping cart—everything," says Tran.

After a few years, Tran decided she needed a change. She learned about Yahoo! Merchant Solutions (then called Yahoo! Stores), and signed on in the beginning of 2001. "The program was easy to use, fairly customizable with a lot of great features, and fully integrated," says Tran. "This was very important to us, because we depend on having a really easy-to-navigate site."

Tran also found a web designer through Yahoo! to help set up the new site. (Yahoo!'s Merchant Solutions website offers a list of web designers who specialize in Yahoo! solutions.) Almost immediately after the new website was set, Tran says she could see the difference: Quite simply, she explains, "We just got more orders."

Yahoo!'s solution was not inexpensive—in fact, at the time, Tran chose the most expensive solution, and she still uses the most expensive one today: Yahoo! Merchant Professional, which costs $299.95 per month plus a nominal one-time setup fee and transaction fees. Also, hiring a web designer generally costs $2,000 to $10,000. Still, that's a lot less than it cost Tran to set up her customized site. "Looking back," says Tran, "I wish I went to Yahoo! first."

eBay

Before taking the plunge and starting a full-fledged website, many online boutique owners test the waters by selling goods on eBay (ebay.com) first. They have good reason: Today, the eBay community includes 276 million registered members from around the world. On an average day, millions of items are listed on eBay. "The most appealing and obvious reason a new business chooses eBay is the access to our enormous customer base," says Jim Griffith, dean of eBay Education at eBay.

To begin selling on eBay, you need to register and create a seller's account, then enter all the details about your item, including price, fixed price payment method, shipping cost, and a photo. Griffith says listing an item is a five-step process that's pretty easy to complete. But he suggests you do your homework before listing items. Research eBay to learn what the current market value is for the types of items you're selling, and what eBay sellers of similar items are doing on the site.

When you list an item on eBay, you're charged an insertion fee. The lowest insertion fee, for items with a starting price of under $1, is 25 cents, and the fee goes up to $4.80 for items that have a buying price of $500 or more. You are also charged a final value fee if your item is sold or purchased. Final value fees start at 5.25 percent of the closing value for items under $25.

Many online boutique owners are also turning to eBay for their online storefront services—especially those already experimenting with eBay. eBay Stores allow you to sell your fixed-price and auction items from a unique destination on eBay. You can build your own eBay Store through an easy series of steps: Create customized categories, include your own logo or choose one of eBay's online images, and list item descriptions and policies.

An eBay Store is promoted to eBay users in several ways: All your listings contain an eBay Store "red door" icon inviting buyers to visit your eBay Store. The eBay Store icon is attached to your user ID for extra visibility. Buyers are also driven to your store through the eBay Store Directory, designed to promote all stores. And you receive your own personalized eBay Store website address to distribute and promote. eBay offers three subscription levels for stores, ranging from $15.95 per month to $299.95 per month.

TOP TEN REASONS TO OPEN AN eBAY STORE

Want to open an eBay store? Proponents say you should because they allow you to

1. control and monitor your inventory.

2. showcase your merchandise.

3. get your own private search engine.

4. cross-promote your items on eBay.

5. reduce eBay selling fees.

6. become visible to search engines.

7. learn from store reports.

8. save time listing and relisting.

9. get marketing help from eBay.

10. improve your image.

Should You Etsy?

Before launching an online boutique, many people selling handmade products turn to Etsy (etsy.com), an online marketplace for buying and selling all things handmade. Since its launch in June 2005 over 100,000 sellers from around the world have opened up Etsy shops. And many online boutique owners are turning to Etsy instead of eBay because they find that it can be difficult to compete with the lower-priced, mass-produced jewelry featured on eBay.

How does selling work on Etsy? For starters, it's free and easy. You simply choose your username and password, then confirm an e-mail address. There's also the extra step of signing up to be a seller after choosing your username. To prevent against fraud, it requires you keep a valid credit card on file. Sellers, be careful when choosing your username because it will also be your

ONLINE SHOPPING SET FREE

Shh! Want to know a secret? There's a little online store company out there that is making a name for itself and actually competing with the likes of eBay Stores and Yahoo! Merchant Solutions. The company is Flying Cart (flyingcart.com), and it is being used by many online boutique owners selling merchandise like clothing and jewelry.

What is its appeal? For starters, the Basic service is free. Anyone with merchandise can start a store, and all that is needed is a PayPal Business account, which is free. (We'll discuss PayPal in a later chapter.) With the free Basic version of Flying Cart, you can post up to five products and have three transactions per month. Because transaction fees are deducted at the time of sale, owning the store remains free until products are selling—stripping away the financial risks of owning an online store.

In general, the stores are professionally designed, easy to navigate, and fun to browse. The company also offers store owners step-by-step guides on how to promote their stores online and one-click submission into Google Product Search (more about this later, as well). In addition, Flying Cart supports SSL (Secure Socket Layer) security so your customers can feel safe, or at least safe, while shopping.

There are other versions of the service. For $15 per month, online boutique owners can post 50 products and have unlimited transactions. For $30 per month, online boutique owners can list an unlimited number of products and have unlimited transactions.

These fees also get store owners additional features, such as an Automatic Google Product Search submission (discussed later), a customer domain name, and the ability to view detailed product statistics to learn which products are selling and which are not.

Perhaps the coolest Flying Cart feature is Store Networking, which allows Flying Cart store owners to network with other stores online so they can promote each other. Basically, this feature works like a webring, a collection of websites around the internet joined together in a circular structure. With webrings, store owners can have links to other websites displayed at the bottom of a site, as they do on Flying Cart.

shop name. Since usernames on Etsy cannot be changed, pause and consider your username carefully.

Then, you can set up your site. Every seller on Etsy gets their own shop for free. It's located at username.etsy.com. For example, if your username is rokali, your shop is at rokali.etsy.com. You can customize your shop by adding a banner, bio, etc.

Next, list your items, which is done in five simple steps. Etsy recommends that you have photos of your merchandise and descriptions ready before jumping in. Listings stay up for four months, and you can include up to five items in your listing. You pay 20 cents for each listing.

For example, if you list one piece of jewelry, it costs 20 cents. If you have three of the same pieces and put them all in the same item listing, it costs 60 cents. After four months, if the item does not sell out, it is unlisted but you may easily relist it if you like (at the same price).

Etsy has also implemented a combined shopping cart. This makes it even easier for sellers to offer discounts on shipping of multiple items. It also makes it easier for buyers to shop from multiple sellers at once.

Sellers can set shipping profiles, complete with different shipping costs for the countries to which they ship their items. These profiles can then be loaded into a listing during the listing process. These profiles can save a tremendous amount of time when listing items.

Etsy sellers now have the ability to create sections in their shops. Items can be categorized into these sections to make shopping easier. Sections are totally customizable.

As a seller, you get to choose what payment methods you accept. Etsy recommends PayPal because it facilitates instant payment and offers antifraud protection. When an item sells, both the buyer and seller are sent e-mails with the transaction details. There's a 3.5 percent sales fee, which does not include the shipping fees. All Etsy fees are paid using the credit card you put on file when signing up as a seller. Each month, Etsy adds up your fees, and on the last day of the month, sends you an e-mail listing everything. You can pay your bill at any time by manually using your credit card on file.

All fees are in U.S. dollars. Etsy, however, says that if someone from another country purchases an item on your site, currency conversion is handled automatically by those services. Etsy also says that it will soon be adding built-in currency conversion.

Etsy says it responds to all reported transactions quickly, and if a buyer does not pay for an item, Etsy will happily refund all fees associated with the transaction, letting you relist it for free.

Etsy's Features

Etsy, in general, is a key way to get your merchandise out there before launching a full-on site. A list of key features includes:

- *Tags.* Tags are keywords used to sort items on Etsy. The first tag on an item determines which top-level category it's listed under. Subcategories on Etsy are also based on tags. For example, the Drawing subcategory inside Art shows items tagged with Art and Drawing. A single tag can be comprised of multiple words, such as Bath and Beauty. You can have up to 14 tags per item.
- *Materials.* Materials are a special kind of single-word keywords. Instead of helping you understand what an item is used for, they help you figure out what it's made out of. You can click a material anywhere you see it and be taken to a list of all other items using the same material. You can list up to 13 materials per item.
- *Conversations.* Also called "Convos" for short, Conversations are an Etsy-only messaging system. It's a great way to communicate with other members, especially regarding the details of a transaction. You can access your Conversations inbox by clicking the link at the very top of the site header. You can send and receive Convos from any other registered member. Additionally, you can set your preferences receive an e-mail notification every time you get a new Convo. Note: If send out several conversations that all have similar content in a short period of time, your conversations are automatically disabled. The best way to communicate with groups, clubs, or send shop announcements and promotions, is to use your business e-mail address. Conversations were designed to handle transaction arrangements.

➡ *Forums.* Forums are a big part of Etsy's community spaces. These are public bulletin boards on Etsy for all members to discuss a variety of things, ranging from getting help with using the site or advice on running a shop to suggesting new site features and reporting bugs, as well as just socializing with others in the Etsy community. The Forums can be found in the Community section of the site.

➡ *Chat rooms.* Chat rooms are interactive spaces where you can virtually talk with other members in real time. There are three standard chat rooms, but members can also create their own custom rooms and even password-protect a room for privacy. A chat room is a great place to socialize with other members and get immediate help. Etsy teams can also use the chat rooms for virtual meetings. The chat rooms can be found in the Community section of the site.

➡ *The Storque.* The Storque is Etsy's online zine. It provides information and announcements for buyers and sellers about the site and the handmade lifestyle. Articles are written by Etsy's staff and members of the Etsy community. It's updated several times daily with new content. Readers can also leave comments on articles.

➡ *Virtual Labs.* These are special multimedia chat rooms. Etsy staff and members can use the Virtual Labs to hold interactive workshops, like seminars on marketing or real-time shop critiques. Scheduled events are announced in the Storque. The Virtual Labs can be found in the Community section of the site.

➡ *Favorites and Hearts.* When customers find an item or shop on Etsy that they love, they can bookmark it by adding it to their Favorites. In Etsy-lingo, this is also called "hearting" an item or shop. To heart an item/shop, click the link in the right sidebar on a shop or item page that says "Add this to favorites." To view a Favorites list, customers go to Your Etsy Favorites. They can also browse the Favorites of other members by clicking the Favorites link in their Profiles. They can also see who has hearted a certain item/shop by clicking the right sidebar link that says, "See who hearts this item/shop."

➡ *Showcase.* The Showcase is a paid advertising program for Etsy shops. Sellers can purchase a spot to promote their items on the site. There are a few different kinds of Showcases on Etsy. The Main Showcase (a.k.a. the Homepage Showcase) is linked from the front page of the site and features items from 36 sellers daily. A one-day spot on the Main Showcase costs $15. The Main Showcase draws from a shop's Featured Items. The Storque Showcase is linked from the front page of the Storque and features items from 25 sellers daily. A one-day spot on the Storque Showcase costs $7. The Storque Showcase draws from a shop's Featured Items. Additionally, there are Category Showcases displayed as a ticker at the top of the main page for each category. These Showcases feature items from 25 sellers daily, selected by the seller from their listings in that category. A one-day spot on a Category Showcase costs $7.

➡ *The Treasury.* It is a member-curated gallery of short-lived lists of 12 handpicked items each. Members can feature their favorite items, items selected on a theme, or just whatever they like. The Treasury is not intended for self-promotion, but instead to acknowledge and share the many cool things for sale on Etsy. Etsy's staff (also known as Etsy Admin) often chooses an exceptional Treasury list to promote on the homepage as handpicked items.

➡ *Shop Local.* Shop Local is a feature that allows browsers to browse through shops in a specific geographic area, like your hometown, state, or country. This site section is based on the optional information sellers provide in their Profiles, so you may need to be creative in your search terms if you live in a town with a common name or a in remote area.

➡ *Pounce.* Pounce is a shopping tool that allows buyers to browse through recently purchased items, and view more great things for sale in the same shop.

➡ *Geolocator.* The Geolocator is a way to search the world for shops in specific locations. You can search by place and a number indicator will pop up on the globe. Click the number and you'll see the avatars for the shops in that location. You can also search for items through the Geolocator, and see from where in the world they will be shipped. This is based on the optional location information sellers provide in their Profiles.

➡ *Colors.* The Colors tool allows you to browse items based on the colors in the listing photos. Just click a dot on the palette and items will pop up. Click the item icon to learn more and visit that shop.

➡ *Time Machine and Time Machine 2.* Both of the Time Machines on Etsy display the 1,000 most recently listed items. The original Time Machine provides different viewing options for items flying through time and space. The TM2 displays items on a grid and allows you to select those that are Recently Listed, Recently Sold, or Expiring Soon.

➡ *Connections.* Connections is a fun way to browse hearted items and see which other Etsy members have taste similar to your own. Connections starts by showing buyers a few of their Favorite items. If they click an item, it will expand to show them who else calls that a Favorite. Click the person icon, and they will see a few of their other Favorite items. They can also search Find User if there's an Etsian you want to start with.

➡ *Suggestions.* The Suggestions feature scans buyers' Favorite items and then displays other items they may like from the Favorites of other members who hearted the same items as them. This is similar to Connections, but only shows the items, not the members who hearted them.

➡ *Gift Guides.* Gift Guides are lists of suggested gifts available on Etsy. These are meant to help shoppers come up with ideas for the perfect gift for that hard-to-buy-for person on their gift lists. These Guides are curated by Etsy's staff. Etsy selects items that are interesting, have great photos and descriptions, and fit one of the Guide themes. Etsy searches the site daily for more items to add to the Guides.

➡ *Feedback.* Buyers may leave a positive or negative feedback rating, a textual comment, and a "Customer Appreciation Photo" for users with whom they've been had a transaction. A feedback score is the cumulative total of all positives (+1) and negatives (–1) sellers receive. The seller can leave feedback as soon as they receive payment, or wait until they've confirmed that the buyer has received the item and is happy with the transaction.

EIGHT REASONS TO USE ETSY

1. You compete with handmade products only.

2. It's only $0.20 to list an item, with a selling fee of 3.5 percent for each item sold.

3. Items are listed for four months.

4. You can upload five photos for each listing for free.

5. You can easily customize your shop to include a banner, profile, and feedback.

6. Payments can be made through PayPal.

7. No confusing auction; set and adjust your prices at your discretion.

8. Etsy submits your store to Google.

➡ *Kiss and Make Up*. This feature offers members the opportunity to change negative feedback if the issue cited has been resolved. Both parties must agree to change the feedback rating from negative to positive. The link for Kiss and Make Up only appears on negative feedback entries for parties involved in a specific transaction. Neutral feedback does not qualify for Kiss and Make Up.

Understanding Online Payment Options

Because you will be selling luxury items online, you need to accept credit card payments for your products. Unfortunately, the information surrounding online credit card purchases is more confusing than any other aspect of marketing on the internet. Note: When you are working with a turnkey e-commerce solution provider, you most likely will be able to sign up for online payments through the solution. But still, it's important to understand how the whole process works.

Basically, you'll need an internet merchant account that lets your customers pay for items with a credit card. The account can be issued by your bank or by a company such as Merchant Warehouse (merchantwarehouse.com). The account will include a setup fee and a percent per transaction fee. If you already have a store or business and a merchant account, you will still need to get an internet account for your online boutique.

You'll need a virtual terminal, which allows you to take phone orders and process the orders securely into your account. It is usually an add-on service that comes with your internet merchant account. You'll also need a payment gateway that allows your customers' credit card data to be secure as they place orders. Leaders in the field are Authorize.net (authorize.net), VeriSign (ww.verisign.com), and SkipJack (skipjack.com).

ALTERNATIVE CREDIT OPTIONS

High-end e-tailers may offer alternative payment options such as Google Checkout and Bill Me Later in place of a traditional credit card payment. By implementing these programs—and finding consumers who will use them—companies can lower their credit card processing costs. To help customers become more comfortable with these alternate methods, some online boutiques are offering special savings when customers use them.

With Google Checkout (checkout.google.com), users can quickly and easily buy from stores across the web and track all of their orders and shipping in one place. Although the service is the new kid on the online payments block, it's gaining users at a fair clip. Google is competing on the basis of low fees for credit and debit card transactions.

The idea behind Bill Me Later is that if customers don't like to enter their credit card on websites or simply don't have them handy, they can still make a purchase by entering only a minimum of info (just their date of birth and the last four digits of their social security number). They get the bill either via the mail or in their inbox if they so choose, and can then pay it as they like. Bill Me Later is offered through CIT Bank, Salt Lake City, Utah, and managed by Bill Me Later, Inc., (bill-me-later.com), a company with expertise in developing and managing payment solutions.

Then, you'll need a shopping cart that allows your customers to shop for merchandise and then check out. Leading cart systems include osCommerce (oscommerce.com), Zen Cart (zencart.com), and 1ShoppingCart (1shopping cart.com).

You may just want to work with a third-party processor, which does all of the processing. Then no merchant account is required. PayPal, an eBay company, is the largest third-party provider and a very popular option. In fact, PayPal says about 150 million people and hundreds of thousands of merchants use its service.

For more details on payment systems, check out the e-commerce primer by John Jantsch on his website, Duct Tape Marketing. Read it here: ducttape marketing.com/article/articles/58/1/An-eCommerce-Primer/Page1.html.

Confidence Boosters

Many consumers are concerned about their data being compromised online, so it's a good idea for you to have a privacy policy—or a link to it—listed squarely on your online boutique to openly explain it to your customers and prospects. After all, privacy and security of consumers' information are very important to online boutique shoppers. When they are buying high-end merchandise, they certainly don't want to have their privacy compromised or their data misused.

At many sites, setting out a primary policy is as easy as putting a link at the bottom of the front page that says "Privacy Policy." When customers or prospects click it, they are delivered to a clear, concise statement of what information is collected from visitors, what's done with it, and if it's made available to other companies, which is not a good idea in today's environment. In fact, studies show that web users are especially sensitive when their data is shared with other sites or businesses. Most seem to feel that if they are interested enough in a site to want to hang around, revealing a bit about themselves is OK, but they do not want that information passed on.

Many online boutique owners turn to privacy promises developed by third parties, such as by the Better Business Bureau Privacy Program (bbbon line.org/privacy) and TRUSTe (truste.com). Program mechanics vary a bit,

PRIVACY PRACTICE

Not sure what to do when it comes to privacy issues and your online boutique? Then check out The Interactive Advertising Bureau's interactive advertising privacy guidelines (iab.net) that were developed recently in a move to preserve consumer privacy. While they were written with advertisers in mind, online boutique owners can use them as a basis for creating a privacy policy. Note: Many online boutique owners turn to lawyers for drafting their privacy statements. You may want to do that as well.

The guidelines include the following:

➡ Consumers should be provided meaningful notice about the information collected and used for interactive advertising.

➡ Consumers should be informed of their choices regarding interactive advertising and empowered to exercise those choices.

➡ Businesses should implement appropriate information security practices.

➡ Businesses should be responsive and accountable to consumers.

➡ Companies should educate consumers about the benefits of interactive advertising.

but the essence is that a business site meets certain basic privacy requirements, pays a fee, and then gets to display a button on the website touting that it fulfills the program's requirements. Some users grumble that these programs don't truly guarantee privacy so much as they promise disclosure of what happens to information surfers reveal, but pretty much everybody agrees that they are a step in the right direction.

To sum up, you should take care to post a link to your privacy policy in a prominent place on your site. In that policy, be clear, simple, and direct. A good strategy is to say, "We sell no information that we collect about you. Never. To anybody." Don't ask questions about visitors' kids—unless there's a compelling and obvious reason to do so. And if you offer visitors free sign-up to e-mail newsletters or sales notices, be quick to remove anybody who asks—preferably on the very day you receive the request. Users grumble a lot about spam, and an easy way to win visitor confidence is to promptly remove anybody from any list upon request.

Winning—and keeping—visitor trust really isn't, and shouldn't be, rocket science. Lots of the same hurdles were overcome years ago by direct mail and catalog sellers. In the case of the internet, plenty of credit card issuers (American Express, Citibank, etc.) are working overtime to encourage their cardholders to make online purchases with the full assurance that the card will protect them from fraud.

And in probably the broadest, most objective look at net privacy issues, the Federal Trade Commission (ftc.org), the lead government agency in the e-commerce arena, has argued that there is no need for government intervention to offer more assurances of privacy and that, on balance, the industry is doing a satisfactory job. For most site operators, this means don't screw up and you'll be able to develop trust on the part of visitors. And once they trust you, they will buy.

Security Seals

There is another kind of seal that online boutiques can add to their sites—security seals. Security seals prove that you're a technologically sound business that isn't going to unintentionally let someone else misuse your information.

Unprotected small businesses face real threats from hackers and phishers looking to steal consumer data. Hacker Safe (hackersafe.com), Thawte (thwate.com), and VeriSign (verisign) and its subsidiaries, including GeoTrust (geotrust.com), all offer services that protect customers' data, improving overall site security. Because such security programs tend to cover a specific part of the e-commerce process—VeriSign, for example, encrypts data while it's in transit, while Hacker Safe protects data that's residing on your computer—businesses may want to consider applying for several.

Security-related seals are as much for your protection as they are for consumers'. In fact, less than 20 percent of consumers say they would shop with a site or company known to be a victim of a data breach, according to research firm JupiterResearch.

The following is an overview of major privacy/security seal programs:

➡ *BBBOnLine.* Certifies that your business is a member in good standing of its local Better Business Bureau and that your site meets set standards, among them, prompt response to consumer complaints and adherence to the BBB's advertising guidelines. It starts at $450.

➡ *GeoTrust.* Certifies that data transmitted to your site is secure and encrypted. Ranges from $249 to $1,499.

➡ *Hacker Safe.* Certifies that your site is tested daily against hacking to protect consumers from identity theft and fraud, and that stored information is encrypted. Ranges from $1,790 to $5,000.

➡ *Thwate.* Certifies that data transmitted to your site is secure and encrypted. Costs $149 to $899.

➡ *TRUSTe.* Certifies that your privacy policy meets set standards, which include notifying consumers how their personal information will be used and giving them a chance to opt-out. Costs $650 to $13,000.

➡ *VeriSign.* Certifies that data transmitted to your site is secure and encrypted. Ranges from $399 to $1,499.

DIAMOND CERTIFICATES

If you are selling diamonds, you might consider providing either AGS (American Gem Society) or GIA (Gemological Institute of America)—two of the world's top labs—certificates. Some online stores offer their own certificates or certificates from other labs. While the AGS/GIA certification is a good idea, not all purchases require certification (most preset diamonds do not come with AGS or GIA certification), and some beautiful diamonds can be bought without certification. Remember, certification doesn't change the quality of the diamond (although and AGS or GIA certificate can add to the value), it certifies the specifications of the diamond.

Keeping Fraudsters at Bay

Many online boutique owners are concerned about fraud—after all, they are selling expensive items. If one sale is fraudulent, they can lose a lot of money. Here are ten tips to keep internet fraudsters at bay:

1. *Carefully review orders.* Whenever you receive an order, review the order carefully. Make sure the consumer filled out all of the information correctly and that it matches. If it is a fraudulent order, in most cases you can catch something that does not seem right by carefully reviewing the entire order.

2. *Check contact, shipping, and credit card information.* The consumer's contact information should match up with the shipping address and the credit card information. If it does not, then you need to find out why they want the products shipped to another address or have a credit card with different contacts. This often, but not always, is sign of a scamster.

3. *Use address verification services.* Provided by most merchant processors, you can run the AVS service on all of your transactions to ensure that the information given matches with the information on the file with the credit card issuing bank. If it is different, then it is possible, among other things, that the consumer has a partner involved with the order. Contacting the consumer to find out the exact reason is highly encouraged.

4. *Watch for free e-mail addresses.* The majority of scamsters use a free e-mail address to hide their identity. It is a good idea to require a real e-mail address from their own domain or their ISP when they order. This can be accomplished by stating the requirement on your order forms.

5. *Document all contacts.* To give yourself greater protection and a bigger fighting chance against fraudulent consumers, document all contacts you have with them. Keep all voice mails and e-mails, along with caller IDs in order to prove your case.

6. *Check domain name records.* One little trick to catch criminals is to look up the domain name records of the domain name they are using in

their e-mail address to see if it matches what was provided in the order. This only works if they have their own website and used their own domain name as the e-mail address. Use the same procedure as explained in tip number 4, and use Network Solutions' database to search for the records. The URL can be found at networksolutions .com/cgi-bin/whois/whois. Their information might not completely match up, depending if something changed or if they are using a

FRAUD REPORT

Is fraud a growing issue? According to the CyberSource Fraud Report for 2008, it is. Key take-away from this year's report include:

➡ Dollar losses from e-commerce fraud continue to grow. Fraudsters will divert approximately $3.6 billion from U.S. e-commerce in 2007, a 20 percent increase over 2006.

➡ The percent of revenue merchants say they will lose to fraud remained stable over 2006 and 2007 (1.4 percent both years), but because e-commerce sales continue to grow, dollar losses to U.S. e-commerce grow proportionately.

➡ Approximately 1.3 percent of accepted orders ultimately turn out to be fraudulent, up from 1.1 percent the year before. But merchants also reject 4.2 percent of U.S. and Canadian orders on suspicion of fraud, and chargeback statistics may represent only half of the actual impact of fraud.

➡ Merchants are increasing the number of fraud detection tools they use to manage payment fraud risk—the largest merchants now use an average of eight.

➡ The cost of fraud containment continues to rise. In 2007, merchants said they were reviewing 27 percent of their orders, up from 23 percent the year before. Of the orders merchants review, three out of four are ultimately accepted as legitimate.

➡ Merchants say orders originating outside the United States and Canada are 2.8 times more likely to be fraudulent. These higher fraud rates could deter some merchants from expanding into this high-growth sector.

business address vs. a home address, but you should get an idea, like it's in the same state or city.

7. *Watch very large orders.* Take special caution when receiving noticeably high orders, especially around holiday seasons. Also pay attention to orders that request overnight delivery. Because the scamsters aren't paying for anything, they do not care about the extra cost; they just want the goods as fast possible.

8. *Use fraudulent order notices.* Place fraudulent order notices, buttons, and images on your order forms and your website content. Let the consumers know that fraudulent orders will be pursued to the fullest extent of the law. By having these notices, you will usually run off most scamsters.

9. *Do telephone searches.* You can purchase a database of phone numbers on a CD or use services such as anywho.com that will do a reverse search on a phone number for you. You can thus confirm the contact information for the phone number the consumer provided.

10. *Call the consumer.* The last, and usually the most effective way, to clear up all confusion is to call the consumer at the phone number they provided. If they gave you a bad phone number, then try contacting them via e-mail for a valid phone number. Be very suspicious about wrong numbers, because most people don't give out wrong phone numbers unless there was a typo.

By using these tips, hopefully you will not fall victim to fraudulent orders. If you are scammed, then take serious action by following the order and prosecuting the fraudulent consumer.

Pay It Safe

Ever hear of the Payment Card Industry Data Security Standard? Get to know it. Not complying with the PCI DSS could cost you big bucks. The PCI standard, a requirement since 2001 that's increasingly being enforced among growing businesses, is intended to help organizations protect customer account data. It includes requirements for security management, policies, procedures, network architecture, software design, and other critical protective measures. Under the

PCI DSS, American Express, MasterCard, Visa, and other credit card associations mandate that merchants and service providers meet certain minimum security standards when they store, process, and transmit cardholder data.

Merchant banks whose retailers don't comply with the PCI standard could be fined up to $500,000—and banks typically pass along penalties. Noncompliant merchants also face losing their card-acceptance privileges. Many smaller online retailers aren't even aware they're out of compliance with PCI until they seek a payment processor. "While merchants should be complying with the standard now, it's going to be [several] months before the card brands start enforcing PCI compliance for the [smaller] merchants, and when they do, it will be more rational than it is now," says Avivah Litan, vice president and director of research at Gartner Inc. in Stamford, Connecticut. "It will be clearer what [smaller merchants] will have to do. They are not going after these guys and fining them now. They are trying to be rational."

Complying with PCI might seem like a hassle, but not complying could bring even bigger headaches, says Martin Elliott, vice president of emerging risk for Visa USA. "The brand damage that can occur to a merchant if their customers' data is compromised can be far more damaging than fees or fines that Visa may assess," he says, offering these tips for complying with the standard.

➡ *Establish a policy on data retention that minimizes the time you hold data.* If you don't need data, delete it.
➡ *Know where your data is stored.* Software can save data in places you may not be familiar with.
➡ *Store only essential data, such as cardholder name, account number, and expiration date, and destroy all obsolete cardholder data.*
➡ *Use only vendors that are also PCI-compliant.*
➡ *Make sure your payment application follows Visa's "Payment Application Best Practices,"* available on Visa's PCI DSS website: usa.visa.com/merchants /risk_management/cisp.html.

The Taxing of Online Sales

If an online boutique owner has a physical presence in a particular state, such as business offices or a warehouse, it must collect sales tax from customers in that state. If a business does not have a physical presence in a state, it is not required to collect sales tax for sales from customers in that state. This may change, however, because of the Streamlined Sales and Use Tax Agreement.

Created in 2002 by the Streamlined Sales Tax Project, the SSUTA aims to make it easier for retailers doing business in multiple states to calculate, collect, and remit existing use tax. While currently a voluntary program, if mandated by law the SSUTA would require businesses to collect and remit sales taxes for the 7,600 different sales tax jurisdictions in this country.

It's hard to say if the SSUTA could become mandatory. For several years, bills to make sales tax collection mandatory have been introduced in Congress—but none have ever been signed into law. But the fact that 19 states have signed on to allow voluntary collection means the movement is gaining traction. What's more, several large, national retailers have negotiated with member states for amnesty deals in return for future collection of sales tax, and more are expected to follow. All this may get the attention of Congress.

To learn more about internet sales tax, check out the following websites:

> *The Sales Tax Institute* (salestaxinstitute.com). Provides a range of services and links associated with sales tax.

> *DavidHardesty.com*. Provides news and feature articles about e-commerce taxation, including e-mail updates from e-commerce expert David Hardesty.

> *Streamlined Sales Tax Governing Board Inc.* (streamlinedsalestax.org). Offers up-to-date information and news about the SSUTA.

CLICK TIP

Want to look up sales tax rates for free? Then go to FreeTaxRates.com from Avalara (avalara.com), a provider of on-demand sales tax calculation services targeting small and mid-sized businesses. There, you will find AvaRates NOW, a free, map-enhanced, rate look-up tool that provides accurate rates for any North American location in real time.

Chapter 7

Inventory and Fulfillment

*Y*ou've done it—you've opened your online boutique in one week (or maybe less). The next step, however, is managing, improving, and ultimately growing your site. Now it is time to examine some of the skills and tasks you'll need to be a successful online boutique owner, such as fulfilling orders, maintaining inventory, and handling customer service. We'll also discuss some next steps in terms of upgrading your site. While all of this is imperative to your business, setting it up may take longer than one week.

Keep in mind, however, that while it's essential to develop well-thought-out strategies for handling every responsibility and task associated with your online boutique's operation, at this point what your customers will be most concerned about is receiving their correctly fulfilled orders in a very timely manner and receiving top-notch customer service.

Inventory

You might think all there is to inventory control is buying merchandise. But like the groceries in your refrigerator and pantry, you have to know what to buy, when to buy it, and how much to buy. If you stock up on 40 loaves of sourdough sauerkraut raspberry bread because it's on sale but your family won't eat it, you've effectively mangled your monthly food budget and lost your customers. They're over next door having supper with the Pinkelmans. On the other hand, if you come home with only two double chocolate macadamia dream cookies and you've got a family of five, you're going to be seriously understocked. You will again have lost your customers, who are down at the corner bakery ruining their dinners with somebody else's desserts.

Catch-22

Your inventory must serve two functions: 1) If you're working with a multiple-product line, it should provide your customers with a reasonable assortment of the products you offer; 2) It should cover the normal sales demands of your company. Now we arrive at the Catch-22 of retail inventory operations. To accurately calculate basic stock, you must review actual sales during an appropriate time period, such as a full year of business. But you don't yet have previous sales and stocking figures to use as a guide. So you will have to use the information from your market research—and your intuition. Keep your ear to the ground and your eyes on your customers' buying habits. Keep good records. Stockpile all this information in your brain's own inventory for future use.

Another factor you'll need to consider in calculating your basic stock is lead time, the length of time between when you reorder a product and when you receive it. Warning: math ahead. Let's say, for example, that you're selling chocolate zeppelins. You know that once you call and place your order, it takes four weeks for the vendor to deliver more zeppelins to you. This means your lead time is four weeks. So if you're selling 10 zeppelins a week, you'll need to reorder before your basic inventory level falls below 40 zeps. If you wait until you're out of zeppelins, you'll also be out of luck, because you'll have to put all those lovely customer requests on back-order and risk losing sales and customers. You'll also lose cash flow. And then you can pronounce "lead" as "led," as in lead-headed. Or hearted.

One way you can protect yourself from inventory shortfalls is by incorporating a safety margin into your basic inventory figures. You can figure safety margins by anticipating external delays or problems. For instance, you might order extra quantities of seasonal merchandise that you know sells quickly, or if you deal with a vendor located in a winter-blizzard zone, you could order extra products before shipping delays set in.

Nightmare on Inventory Street

A word of caution: Some online boutique owners get so excited about a new product that they order entirely too many at one time. Excess inventory creates extra overhead, and that costs you money. Inventory that sits in your garage or warehouse doesn't generate sales or profits.

Online boutique owners sometimes add financial insult to injury by marking overstocks at reduced prices, hoping for a quick sale. This solves the overstock problem but plays havoc with your bottom line because that product you've written into your financial plan as selling at $100 is now pulling in only $50. It's not holding up its share of the weight.

You may be tempted to bounce back from this nightmare by getting timid with your next orders. Don't do this, either. When you reduce normal reordering, you risk creating a stock shortage, and that's not healthy for your bottom line.

We've told you everything not to do, but what makes a good inventory plan? Try the following:

➡ Do as much research as you can before ordering so that you can order as realistically as possible.

➡ Order only what you feel confident will sell. Establish a realistic safety margin.

The Holiday Season

As an online boutique owner selling luxury goods, you'll probably find that your business is seasonal. The holidays, for example, are the busy season. For some online boutique owners, 50 percent of their business takes place right after Thanksgiving and through the holidays.

There's more to a "good season" catalog than just more orders. There are also price differences. Oftentimes, there might be higher-end products in a fall catalog vs. a summer one—so you tend to make more money on your products at that time.

CLICK TIP

Although most online boutiques have seasonal peaks and valleys, it pays to brainstorm ways to keep your customers buying during the lulls. Can you run a special sale or devise an off-season campaign to encourage purchases? Get creative!

Shipping and Handling

You've got your inventory squared away. Now you need to think about how you're going to get it to your customers. Fulfillment—speeding that package from your garage or warehouse to your customer's door—is perhaps the single most important thing you can do in your operation aside from effective marketing. Failure to provide prompt fulfillment results in more complaints, cancellations, and nightmares than just about anything else in the mail order entrepreneur's world.

So exactly how will you get those packages to your customers? You've seen the TV commercials. Your main choices are the USPS (USPS.com), United Parcel Service (ups.com), FedEx (fedex.com), and DHL (dhl.com), which has recently become a major competitor.

The prices these companies charge shipping your packages is based on several criteria, including the quantity of packages you ship on an ongoing basis (volume discounts apply), the shipping services you use, the size and weight of each package, your geographic location, and the destination of each package.

To save money, you'll definitely want to compare rates among the popular couriers. In many situations, quoted prices to ship an identical package are vastly different. You can also save money by dropping off your packages at a FedEx, UPS or DHL location, rather than scheduling a pick-up.

CLICK TIP

To quickly compare shipping rates amongst various couriers, visit iship.com/priceit/price.asp, redroller.com/shippingcenter/home, or pakmail.com/estimator.

Keep in mind that most shipping companies provide shippers with free supplies (envelopes, boxes, labels, etc.). This is also true for the USPS if you ship using its Priority Mail or Express Mail services.

Part of the success of your business will depend on your ability to create and manage a "shipping department" in order to quickly, efficiently, and cost-effectively process and ship orders to your customers. Having ample shipping supplies and forms on-hand will save you time.

If you'll be shipping packages with the USPS, consider investing in a postage machine or using the Click-N-Ship service to avoid constant trips to the local Post Office to purchase postage. You can also set up a planned pick-up when using this service. Check the USPS website for details about online postage service.

CLICK TIP

It might not be critical for small pieces of costume jewelry, but if your customer buys a $4,000 engagement ring online, they'll want to know that you (and your supplier) are using insured carriers (such as FedEx and UPS) and that all shipments are insured for the full value of their contents. So make sure to do this, and to let them know.

If you'll be using the USPS to do the majority of your shipping, Endicia.com (for Mac users, visit mac.endicia.com) offers postage printing/shipping software that uses a DYMO LabelWriter printer (or any laser or inkjet printer) to print U.S. postage and mailing labels with ease. There's a low monthly fee associated with this time-saving service.

Most online boutiques use UPS for packages because it's generally cheaper than FedEx, faster than the post office, and has better tracking capabilities. It pays to comparison shop.

Of course, it's smart business to offer your customers a choice of shipping services. You can tell them, for instance, that you can have their package out to them by Priority Mail with an expected—but not guaranteed—delivery time of three business days. Then you can offer second-day service by UPS or overnight by FedEx at an extra cost. Give the customer options. This way people know you're working with them, in terms of both price and speed. What a great company!

Understanding how the relationship between your business and shipping companies affects customers will go a long way toward keeping your shipping operations on an even keel. In short, your customers will hold you responsible for any delay in receiving their merchandise, even if the delay is caused by the shipping company. So be prepared to be sympathetic to complaining customers—and stern with the USPS, UPS, and FedEx.

Pass the Popcorn

There's a method to everything, including packing and shipping. Here's a list of smart tips for merchants to help you help yourself and your customers.

➡ *Take a tip from the box boy down at the supermarket.* Place heavier or larger items on the bottom of the box and lighter ones on top.

➡ *After you've got each piece of merchandise in the box, place a piece of cardboard on the very top.* This way, if your customer gets carried away with their penknife while slicing open the box, for example, they won't slash their brand-new goodies as well.

➡ *Use shredded newspaper or actual (unbuttered!) popcorn instead of Styrofoam peanuts.* Your customers will appreciate your concern for the environment, and if you get hungry while packing, you can eat your materials!

➡ *Indicate which end of the box should be opened first or face up.* Sometimes breakable merchandise will make an entire cross-country trip in one piece, only to smash on the customer's floor because he opened it wrong side up.

➡ *Make sure your shipping label is clearly visible to the deliverer.* Some shipping companies refuse to deliver a package if any part of the address is obscured or too small to read.

➡ *Absolutely do not ship to a post office box.* Most shipping firms cannot deliver to one. Make sure your order takers ask for an actual street address.

➡ *Include all invoices, receipts, thank-you letters, new catalogs and other printed materials in one envelope with the customer's name on it, placed on top of the merchandise.* This saves your customer the time and frustration of having to dig through packing materials to find them.

➡ *Re-use boxes.* It's not only ecologically sound but also economically smart. When you reuse a box, make sure all old labels, addresses, and postage markings are covered up. Stick another label on top so the delivery person doesn't mix up for whom your package is intended.

➡ *Design packing models so your shippers (and you) know how products fit into boxes; how merchandise is folded, stacked or tissue-wrapped; and how packing materials are used.* Weigh each packing model on a scale and make sure it doesn't go even one-eighth into the next pound. This cuts postage costs, reduces returns from damaged goods, and adds to your income by creating happy repeat customers.

Fulfillment Outsourcing

Outsourcing fulfillment is often smart business. One advantage of using a fulfillment outsourcer (especially one of the larger ones) is that it is able to buy shipping materials in large quantities in order to receive volume discounts. It can then pass the savings on to its clients. Another plus is when you outsource fulfillment, you don't have to run a large warehouse operation, and this in itself can be a big money-saver. (Remember: Buying large amounts of inventory and having that inventory sit is very inefficient and costly.) Perhaps the greatest advantage is that an outside fulfillment organization is likely to be automated. The contractor who has invested millions of dollars to create a system that's highly accurate keeps your costs down, speeds up your processing time, and lowers your inventory requirements. It can do this because it doesn't use a paper-based system, one where a warehouse employee takes a piece of paper and walks through the warehouse picking out each product on the order. This approach is naturally prone to error. Its biggest failure is poor picking. A sophisticated fulfillment operation has an automated system with bar code readers to ensure a higher degree of accuracy.

When you select a fulfillment service, keep in mind:

➡ *Fulfillment is connected with everything else in your operation.* Select an outsourcer that understands the integration involved.
➡ *Make sure you get periodic reports on everything that goes into and out of the fulfillment center.*
➡ *Your fulfillment contractor should be able to handle multiple sales channels.* Regardless of where the orders originate, fulfillment should be able to take place at the same speed and with the same level of efficiency across the board. Furthermore, you should be able to get a channel breakdown report.
➡ *Find out about returns management.* Can the fulfillment company handle returns to your satisfaction? Some providers can even take returned products and refurbish them for you. Some full-service fulfillment

contractors also operate call centers, where they can take orders on your behalf and field customer service calls.

Return Issues

One issue you will see more and more as you expand your business is returns. It's part of the charted territory of online sales. The reasons for returns are as varied as human nature:

➡ People change their minds.
➡ They order the wrong size or wrong color.
➡ They give gifts that aren't quite right (or are entirely wrong).
➡ They order so late that they no longer need the product by the time it arrives.

TRIED AND TRUE

Over the years, online boutique owners have adopted these tried-and-true methods of processing returns:

➡ Instruct customers to ship products back in the original packing materials within 30 days. This ensures that (a) you won't receive returned merchandise years later, and (b) you know the merchandise came from your company instead of somebody else's.

➡ Offer an exchange program in which the customer phones in their concern, and you immediately ship out a replacement product. When the customer receives the replacement, they put the damaged original into the same box the replacement came in, with the same packing materials, and sends it back to you with shipping prepaid by you.

➡ Some companies, for example Lands' End, offer an open return policy. They'll take back anything for any reason any day of any year. You'll have to think carefully about whether you can afford to handle a program like this.

➡ They receive the wrong merchandise, or it arrives in less than pristine condition.

No matter what your customer's reason is, you will have to deal with it—preferably in a win-win manner. You should have a return policy already in place and clearly stated in all your advertising material. If you've decided on a no-return policy, you must spell it out in your advertising and/or catalog so that, hopefully, the customer already knows this when ordering. If you've got a limited-return policy, you must clearly write this out in your advertising and ordering materials. Stick to your policy, but remember that you want to keep your customer happy. If bending the rules a bit might make the difference between a repeat customer and one who chooses never to use your company again, you know what to do.

Many Happy Returns

What's commonly included in a limited return policy? You might accept returns only on certain products, within a certain time period (say 30 days), with certain tags still attached, or (often in the case of CDs, DVDs, or software) with the product packaging unopened.

HAPPY RETURNS, HAPPY CUSTOMERS

Want to make your customer happy? Then make your returns process easy. According to the fourth annual survey sponsored by Austin, Texas-based returns processor Newgistics Inc. (newgistics.com), for the third year in a row, at least nine out of ten direct shoppers (90 percent) cited a convenient returns policy as very important, important, or somewhat important in deciding to shop with a new or unknown online or catalog retailer. Additionally, most respondents (69 percent) said they are not likely to shop again with a direct retailer if the return process is inconvenient. What's more, 68 percent of respondents said the ability to make a return from home was very important or important when deciding whether to shop with an online or catalog retailer.

Think carefully about how you structure your return policy. More and more retail stores are allowing customers to try out products and then return them within 14 to 30 days. If you go for a policy like this, you could be asking for a lot of unusable, returned stock. On the other hand, you can garner a reputation as a friendly, here-to-please company that customers will want to buy from. And you can always offer those "test-driven" products at a discount, earning yourself happy customers of a slightly different bent. Also, check with your vendors; you may be able to send your returns back to them.

Customer Service for Success

If there's a mantra for online boutique owners, it's this: Customers may be virtual, but their dollars are real. Nowadays, consumers expect a high-level of service from online retailers. How can you use customer service as a completive advantage? Just follow these steps.

- ➡ *Anticipate questions.* Many online boutique owners anticipate questions and then answer them in their FAQs. Doing this will save your and your customers' time. Of course, sometimes customers will e-mail you with questions, and this can be a good thing. Getting lots of e-mail complaining about a certain feature that the customer has simply misunderstood or bemoaning the lack of a particular product that you know is in stock, lets you learn important things about how your site is failing to communicate to visitors. As e-mail comes in, don't ever look for how the e-mailers are wrong. Look for ways to reshape your site to eliminate user problems (even the ones they only imagine they have).

- ➡ *Answer questions quickly.* Some online boutique owners swear they respond to customer e-mails within four hours—and this is a goal of many e-commerce firms. But what is right for you? With a smaller staff (and probably no staff during night hours), you might find a 24-hour

> **CLICK TIP**
>
> Do it now: Create a place for FAQs on your site ASAP. View your FAQs as a work in progress. You'll continually update and expand them as more customer concerns and needs come to light.

standard to be enough of a challenge. But monitor customers. If they demand faster response, somehow you have to find a way to meet their needs.

➡ *Stay in touch.* A week or two after any order is filled, e-mail your customers and ask if they would recommend your online boutique. "No" answers will hurt, but follow up on every one because these are the people who will tell you what you need to do to build a winner of a website. Given how awesomely powerful this simple tool is, it's stunning that more online boutiquers haven't jumped on it. Don't make the same mistake. To win these "no" customers, responding quickly is just one piece of the puzzle. Evaluate and prioritize the collected customer feedback to address key customer needs, and then implement new features to the website that improve the online shopping experience for existing and new customers.

➡ *Hold their hands.* Understand your customers' needs, and be ready to help. Be patient, too. Any customer can become your best customer, because they will shop only where they feel comfortable—and if your online boutique makes it on that shortlist, watch the orders tumble in.

➡ *Stay sensitive.* A worry with e-mail is that it's easy to seem cold and unresponsive in the formality of the written word. Read and reread your responses before they go out. You want to be—and appear—interested in the customer's issues and eager to find solutions.

➡ *Aim higher.* In the online space, the service bar is being lifted ever higher. At a minimum, you must have 24/7 phone support, as well as functionality like real-time chat and personalization that enables you to better meet your customers' needs.

Netiquette: A Guide to Communicating Clearly on the Internet

This may be a good time go over the rules of netiquette—the proper ways to communicate with others online or in e-mail exchanges. Let's face it: Communicating online—in your business or personally—without creating misunderstandings is a challenge. One problem is there aren't any facial expressions, body language, or environment to help you express yourself.

Another problem is that there is little "give and take" for developing what you mean to say or are discussing.

When dealing with customers—or friends, family, and co-workers—it's best to follow these simple rules of netiquette:

➡ *Be clear.* Make sure the subject line (e-mail) or title (web page) reflects your content.

➡ *Use appropriate language.* If you have a question on whether or not you are too emotional, don't send the message, save it, and review it later. No one can guess your mood or see your facial expressions, etc. All readers have are your words, and your words can express the opposite of what you feel.

➡ *Don't use all capital letters.* It's the equivalent of shouting or screaming.

➡ *Be brief.* If your message is short, people will be more likely to read it.

➡ *Make a good impression.* Your words and content represent you. Review/edit your words and images before sending.

➡ *Be selective about e-mail or site information.* Information on the internet is very public and can seen by anyone in the world, including criminals, future employers, and governments.

➡ *Forward e-mail messages you receive only with permission of the sender.*

➡ *You are not anonymous.* What you write in an e-mail and on a website can be traced back to you.

CLICK TIP

Communicating online with your customers and site visitors doesn't have to be impersonal. Instant chat is a quick way to let website visitors reach you or your staff to handle support issues or answer questions. Free, ad-supported instant chat service Gabbly (gabbly.com) can also act as a forum where your site visitors interact with each other. It can be slightly customized for size and is a copy-and-paste step away from embedding in your site. It's an interesting example of how easy it can be to add chat and a dash of social networking to your website or business blog. Also look into chat service Karzi.com (karzi.com), currently in beta.

CLICK TIP

Take a tactic used by the slick catalog companies. When you haven't heard from a customer in a while, drop them an e-mail: "Have we disappointed you in any way? We would really value your feedback." Maybe the customer is indeed irked with you; maybe not. Either way, the e-mail will remind the customer that you are a store that cares.

➡ *Consider others.* If you are upset by what you read or see on the internet, forgive bad spelling or stupidity. If you think it violates the law, forward it to the FBI or your state's Attorney General.

➡ *Obey copyright laws.* Don't use others' images, content, etc. without permission. Also, don't forward e-mail, or use website content without permission. Visit the Library of Congress' Guide on "Copyright Basics."

➡ *Cite others' work.* Refer to the Guide on "Citation."

➡ *Use distribution lists appropriately and with permission.*

➡ *Do not send spam.* Spam is posting or sending unsolicited e-mail, often advertising messages, to a wide audience.

➡ *Don't forward chain letters.* If you receive one, notify your web master.

➡ *Don't respond to "flames" or personal attacks.* If you receive one, contact your web master for action and referral.

If you follow these rules in your online boutique dealings in general, you should be fine.

These steps will get you started delivering better customer service, but they are not enough. Successful entrepreneurs say that the only way to do online service right is to have the right attitude, really believe the customer is king, and make sure that every customer service reps knows it. Many fail on this score, but when you've made customer service your top and continuing priority, success is within reach. Don't get seduced by the notion that the websites with the best technology will inevitably win. Usable, reliable technology is a must, but where the real e-tailing battlefield will be is in service. That's the irony about e-tailing: At the end, what prevails online is what prevails off-line: consistent, respectful, considerate service.

STELLAR CUSTOMER SERVICE: DO YOU HAVE WHAT IT TAKES?

The great thing about the internet is that anyone can set up shop. Of course, that also means you now have to compete with the big guys—and customer service is no exception. "Customers today are very savvy," says Lauren Freedman, president of the e-tailing group inc. (e-tailing.com), an e-commerce consulting firm in Chicago. "They expect best-of-breed customer service everywhere they shop on the web. They don't care if you are smaller."

Each year, Freedman's firm tracks the top 100 e-tailers on 11 criteria relative to customer service and communication. The most successful online businesses offer the following:

1. *A toll-free number*. "This is pretty critical today," says Freedman. "If a small business doesn't offer this now, it should think about it."

2. *Keyword search*. According to Freedman, "People today are used to searching for things online, and they want a seamless search experience on the websites they are considering buying from."

3. *Timely answers to e-mail questions*. "A small e-tailer should probably strive for 48 hours," says Freedman, who adds it's important to personally address customer queries vs. sending automated responses.

4. *Four or fewer days to receive a package via ground shipping*. "A small e-tailer should try to strive for five business days," says Freedman. "And they should make it very clear—in all their communications with their customers—what their shipping policies are."

5. *Six or fewer clicks to checkout*.

6. *Inventory status*. While real-time status is best, "[Let] your customer know within 24 hours if the product they are ordering is in stock or is not in stock," says Freedman.

7. *Online shipping status*. "[Offer] a link to UPS or FedEx so they can check their orders on their sites," says Freedman.

STELLAR CUSTOMER SERVICE: DO YOU HAVE WHAT IT TAKES?, CONTINUED

8. *Order confirmation in the shopping cart.*

9. *An e-mail order confirmation with the order number included.*

10. *Recommendations for other products and features during the shopping process.* "This is a standard for the larger merchants, but something that small e-merchants should strive for," says Freedman, who adds doing so can help you increase order size.

11. *Clearly displayed customer service hours.* This is especially important if you have limited customer service hours, says Freedman.

Try doing something extra special for your customers. For example, if you are selling jewelry, why not put the merchandise in a cotton-padded gift box or a satin-tie pouch? Also, let customers know what you did in the e-mail you send letting them know that their merchandise is on its way. You could say, "I included a gift box to protect your fresh water pearls necklace." Once they're aware of it, they'll think "how nice" or "how special" you are, or "This is great, now I don't need to gift wrap."

Just try doing something extra for your customers and see if it doesn't make a difference. Going the extra mile shows them you care not just about their purchase, but also about their enjoyment of owning and wearing your merchandise. And remember: Personalized customer service like this could just keep them coming back for more.

It's Your Call

You know how important good customer service is to the success of your online boutique, so why not take it up a notch with click-to-call technology? This feature, which has grown more affordable and popular thanks to VoIP, gives customers real-time support, differentiates your site from the competition, and can boost sales, too.

Click-to-call makes it easy for customers to connect directly with a sales or customer service agent: They simply click an icon on your site and input their phone number. Within a few seconds, they receive a call from an agent, who can provide a guided online experience and even suggest complementary items and relevant offers based on the caller's information.

Click-to-call providers include Art Technology Group's eStara subsidiary (estara.com), LivePerson Inc.(liveperson.com), and LiveOffice LLC (liveoffice.com). Prices vary. LivePerson's click-to-call service, LiveCall, for example, offers live chat, e-mail management, and FAQ, and costs about $150 per month. LiveOffice's service costs 10 cents per minute for each call completed. eStara's higher-end product charges a setup fee that costs several thousand dollars and a licensing fee based on call volume.

Headsets.com Inc.
Mike Faith, CEO and President
Location: San Francisco, California
Year Started: 1998

Meet an entrepreneur who has built a successful online business—and is watching it grow every year. Mike Faith, of Headsets.com Inc., a leading provider of headsets through its website Headsets.com (headsets.com) has been consistently successful. While the site may not be considered a pure "online boutique," you can learn a lot about what it takes to start a successful online business that sells a nice product from him.

Please tell me about your background. Why did you start Headsets.com? When was it founded?

Mike Faith: I emigrated to the United States from England, where the business climate is so stifling that it felt like "entrepreneur" was a dirty word. I wanted the freedom to do business in a way that supported my creativity, and the United States seemed like the perfect place. So in 1990, I jumped on a plane and never looked back. I started a few ventures, which were moderately successful. They taught me some of the fundamentals of running a business, and generated enough capital for me to start Headsets.com in 1998. Those early companies were call-center based, and so we used a lot of telephone headsets. Finding good quality units at a reasonable cost and with decent supplier support, turned out to be harder than it should have been, impossible in fact, and that tripped my opportunity radar.

How much money did you start Headsets.com with? Did you get venture capital money? Was it self-funded?

Faith: Six weeks after realizing the opportunity, and $40,000 of my own money, we were in business selling headsets. It was 1998, and we had a single product. The simplicity and cost of our offering was an instant hit, and we quickly grew revenues to the point that I was comfortable putting up the shutters on my other businesses to concentrate on the opportunity. Two years later, in 2000, our competitors were slashing prices and their margins. We were losing our differentiator. We looked at our business and the original opportunity, and realized we had only served two of the three needs of the market, a good product, at a low cost—we were missing that vital third part—service. So in 2000, as we incorporated from an LLC, we accepted a small round of funding, and that allowed us to fund a cultural shift in the organization, to deliver what we think is world-class customer service.

Where did you open up shop? Why?

Faith: My wife and I were living in San Francisco when I started the business, and so naturally that's where we opened up shop. The Bay Area is a wonderful region with a near endless pool of world class talent and an attitude to business innovation that for me at least, captures all the reasons I moved to the United States. Many times, over the years, people have questioned the premiums we pay running a call center in the middle of one of the most expensive cities in the country, but every time it comes up, we can't help but see it as a strength. If you want the best, you have to pay for it. We want the very best!

What's been the biggest challenge you've had in building your company?

Faith: The biggest challenge we've faced, I'm proud to admit, has been my own growth. I'm an entrepreneur, I make decisions like you'd expect me to, and I've had to learn to involve others, think longer term and more strategically, and deal with a lot more formality and "corporate stuff" than I'm used to. It took awhile before I built a team that I could trust to share the load, to execute with my vision and my passion. Now we are just crossing that 50-employee threshold, and our challenges are to continue to build a strong, robust organization, that is growing at 50 percent annually, without losing those things that made us successful: our adaptability, agility, and efficiency. It's a challenge I relish.

How have you broadened your offerings or diversified your company since starting out? Why is this important for e-tailers to do?

Faith: I'm going to give you an answer that perhaps will go against conventional wisdom. The world's greatest marketer, Al Ries, taught me about ruthless focus years ago—and it's been an invaluable lesson. We sell headsets, and we only sell headsets. Because of this, we know more about selling headsets than anybody else, and we sell more headsets than anybody else. The more headsets we sell, the better we get at it. It's a wonderful virtuous cycle. I believe that other e-tailers would do well to stay focused, do less, do it better, and reach deeper into a narrower market.

Of course, we've been tempted to diversify—we have this fantastically efficient, high service model for selling business-to-business productivity tools—why shouldn't we apply that to as many products that fit the mold as possible? Well, we dabbled in a few areas, but found that even trying to pick up incremental sales in similar categories like audio headphones and telephone conferencers complicated our business to the point that the whole became less than the sum of the parts, not more.

Many people warn us of disruptive technologies, or saturated markets and we aren't cavalier or arrogant enough to believe that these risks aren't real. They are, but for us to tackle these risks through diversification means abandoning our core strengths, and that's just not an acceptable trade.

Who is your competition? Are they big guys? If so, how do you find your niche against them?

Faith: You can get headsets from lots of places, but its almost always part of a diverse offering of products. A headset is still for the most part a consultative sale, despite their widespread adoption and the simplicity of the product relative to other things on the corporate desktop. So we make sure we remain true to our company tagline "America's Headset Specialists," and we serve the markets needs better than generic telecoms suppliers, or office equipment suppliers who try and bolster volume by slashing margins and the all-important expert knowledge and service. For the longest time we were the little guys, carving out a niche with the small companies and new headset users, while our big rivals squabbled over the large call-center market. But now we look around the competitive landscape and find the call-center market dwindling as it moves increasingly offshore and new headset adoption in the small office sector driving all the growth in the industry, with us leading the charge and the historic big-guns standing eerily silent. It's exhilarating.

Have you thought about going public? Why or why not?

Faith: I've often thought of taking Headsets.com public, but I usually talk myself out of it the same day. Then a month later, I'll think of it again. The shift to a public company would change our business and our ability to compete on the terms that I know will win. Public companies maintain their stock price by focusing on growth. But like success and happiness, growth is a byproduct of doing something to the best of your ability. The pursuit of growth for growth itself will always come up short. As a private company, we are free to focus on delivering what the customer wants: the best product at the best price, and with the best service. The irony is, of course, by not focusing on growth, we are enjoying it in abundance, around 50 percent annually.

How do you market your site? What works? What hasn't?

Faith: We don't market our site specifically. Our website, as proud of it as we are, is nothing more than a way for our customers to place an order as quickly and efficiently as possible. We do market our products, of course (which ultimately drives traffic to our web servers and our call center) and we do that through a pretty significant business-to business-direct mail program using a catalog and solo product offerings. We also use pay-per-click online advertising, do phenomenally well in natural search rankings and have a lively affiliate program. Of course, it helps that our company name (Headsets.com) and

800 number (800 Headsets) say pretty much everything you need to know to find us and what we sell. But above all of our marketing efforts, we've found that we've reached a critical mass, with repeat and referral business now becoming our largest source.

How do you up your look-to-buy ratio?

Faith: We simply remove all the barriers to buying our products. I know that sounds trite, but it's true. We offer great prices, unbeatable guarantees, a solid reputation, free trial of our products, all backed up by knowledgeable, smart, professional reps offering the world's best customer service. I challenge anyone who needs a headset to not buy from us. Why would you go anywhere else? Hey, even I want to buy a headset from us, and I'm a skeptic!

Time for an Upgrade?

Wait, didn't you just finish building your online boutique? And haven't we covered how to successfully grow and manage it? Yes, but the reality is that as your online business grows, you will find that you need to upgrade your website sooner rather than later. In fact, in an effort to respond to customer demands, more and more web merchants are spending more and more money upgrading their e-commerce platforms.

There are many ways you can upgrade your site. For example, if you are using a hosted solution, you can upgrade to a higher level plan. Or you can

SECRETS TO SUCCESS

What is Headsets.com's secret weapon against some of the bigger companies that sell headsets? For one, they are experts. Headsets are all they sell. In addition, they offer great prices, unbeatable guarantees, a solid reputation, and free trial of products—all backed up by knowledgeable, smart, professional reps offering what Faith calls the "world's best customer service." These are all weapons any small e-tailer or online business owner can use to compete against the big guys—and win.

CLICK TIP

You don't have to spend a lot of money on a big, traditional mass media adverting campaign to be successful. Look at Headsets.com: It sends out targeted, business-to-business direct mail catalogs and uses search engine marketing. Of course, it helps that it also has a memorable name (Headsets.com) and an 800 number (800 Headsets) that says pretty much everything you need to know about them!

move from a do-it-yourself solution to an outsourced solution. Or you can do it the other way around.

One company that has decided to upgrade its site is Giggle, a New York-based retailer that sells upscale baby gear in four stores (two in New York and two in San Francisco) as well as through its website, giggle.com. The company, with revenues of over $10 million, was founded in 2003 by Ali Wing. A small website went up shortly thereafter.

In April 2006, however, Wing upgraded her website. It now has a fully scalable e-commerce platform. "This site was a big change for us," says Wing. "We now have a platform in place that is fully scalable and that is a true retail channel for us. Going forward, lots of technical functionality will keep being released." For example, Wing says the company will continue to invest in "easy-shop tools such as check lists."

Wing says the company also invests a lot in photography. "That's the most expensive part of being online, because the expense of keeping product databases current and photos that translate really well to make them easy to shop online is not easy."

To launch the site, Giggle switched to a new web development partner. And instead of outsourcing the entire project to the firm, Giggle does some of it in-house.

Virid (virid.com), an interactive services agency in Reston, Virginia, developed the new giggle.com site with giggle based on Virid's Covella e-commerce platform. "Basically we do the art and design and user interface," says Wing. "They make it work that way and host it."

SPEED UP YOUR ONLINE BOUTIQUE WITH AJAX

Want to increase the interactivity, speed, and usability of your web pages? AJAX could be the answer. Short for Asynchronous JavaScript and XML, AJAX is a web development technique for creating interactive web applications. In general, it makes web pages feel more responsive by exchanging small amounts of data with a server behind the scenes so an entire web page does not have to be reloaded each time the user makes a change.

The benefits are obvious to Fairytale Brownies in Chandler, Arizona, which has implemented AJAX to speed up the checkout process on its site. Founded in 1992 by childhood friends Eileen Joy Spitalny and David Kravetz, Fairytale Brownies is the nation's leading purveyor of mail-order gourmet brownies, with sales projections of over of $8 million.

When the company redesigned its website to make its brownies look more appealing, it used AJAX to speed up the gift list checkout section. "This gift list shows our customers who received gifts from them before," explains Spitalny. "It's a very popular feature, but we wanted to make it as quick and easy to use as possible."

Before AJAX, any change to addresses, ship dates, quantities, or gift messages meant waiting for entire web pages to reload. But AJAX loads pages only once; changes need only small data updates. This translates into a smoother process that benefits not only customers but also employees, who spend less time on the phone with customers.

Fairytale employed an outside consultant to implement AJAX. Spitalny suggests finding a programmer who is familiar with JavaScripting and XML. She also suggests a visit to ajax.asp.net, a Microsoft site that provides free tutorials and starter kits to help programmers understand the technology.

Before implementing an AJAX redesign, however consider the following tips from David Fry, founder, president, and CEO of Fry Inc., an e-commerce design, development, and managed services provider in Ann Arbor, Michigan.

SPEED UP YOUR ONLINE BOUTIQUE WITH AJAX, CONTINUED

➡ *Perform a usability test.* Determine your goal in using AJAX and then select a small audience to try it on. If it likes it, expand AJAX's use.

➡ *Make sure AJAX doesn't affect your search rankings.* AJAX can distort search rankings because web crawlers have to parse the information differently. To get around that, you'll have to work with someone experienced with the issue.

➡ *Be aware that AJAX performs differently with different browsers.* Internet Explorer 7 is AJAX-friendly, but if you code your site to be compatible with IE7, it might not be compatible with IE6.

Wing says Giggle launched the new site this because "we were ready to take the next step. Until now we didn't have the right platform that we thought could scale with the demands of our business." For example, Giggle prides itself on its customer service, so the site had to meet its high standards.

"Anybody who thinks the online piece is cheap and easy just hasn't done it a lot," says Wing. "It is 24 by 7 selling, which means that data has to always be right, product has to always be right, everything has to be current, the site always has to be updated, and you have to be able to respond to

CLICK TIP

Instead of upgrading your site, you might want to launch a microsite that lets you focus on a specific purpose, such as selling clearance or discounted items, products to businesses (vs. consumers), new merchandise that's complementary to your core products, or even a tryout for a whole new product line. Before building one, however, consider the costs. Building a microsite costs essentially the same as setting up a traditional website—from $2,500 to $50,000 or more, depending on the sophistication. In addition, a microsite may require additional employees. Before launching one, make sure the same results cannot be achieved using your current web infrastructure.

however people are reacting to you. From an infrastructure perspective—and also an organizational one—we didn't have a platform that could support the demand."

Unlike other online boutique owners, Wing says upgrading the site didn't cost her any more money than her previous iteration. "To do what we were doing third-party was much more expensive for the results," says Wing. "What I am actually spending for the results I am getting now is at worst commensurate. I am not spending any more since we did this upgrade. I'm just spending it differently and more effectively."

Searchandising

As many online boutique owners grow their sites, they begin to employ new and improved ways for visitors to search their sites. One technique is called "searchandising," which allows online boutique owners to list results from related searches as well as related products, including those purchased by other shoppers; derive customer analytics data from site search activity; and personalize search results based on the purchase histories of unique customers or customer segments.

Faceted navigation, which segments products into manageable categories, is also worth exploring. Basically, faceted navigation plays on a shopper's inclination to start with a vague idea of what they're looking for and browse until they stumble on relevant products.

Celebros (celebros.com), Mercado Software (mercado.com), and SLI Systems (sli-systems.com) offer searchandising solutions for entrepreneurs. Each takes a slightly different approach, and costs vary—SLI's product, for example, is about $10,000 annually, while Mercado's runs about $3,500 per month.

Achieving optimal results from a searchandising program means:

➡ *Planning ahead.* Search and navigation are inextricably tied. To have an efficient search system, you need an effective navigation scheme. In short, if your site is unorganized, it makes information discovery difficult.

➡ *Feeding search data into merchandising strategies.* Studies show 68 percent of best-in-class companies use consumer-generated search data in their merchandising tactics to influence results.

➡ *Measuring conversions resulting from search.* This is key to understanding which search results lead to sales and which tactics fail. Fifty-five percent of best-in-class retailers actively monitor conversion rates achieved from search optimization tactics and continually fine-tune results as a corrective measure.

Going Wireless

You also may want to explore making your online boutique mobile-friendly. With more and more people using the internet with their mobile phones, more and more sites are launching mobile-optimized versions of their service. And, more and more affluent users are using their mobile phones for traditional web activities, including shopping.

Most people venturing into these waters set up a separate, mobile version of their website, which they advertise—and users can click through to—on their home page. A word of advice: If you are planning to make a mobile-optimized version of your site, make sure to speak with an expert first. Do an online search for "wireless web" or "mobile websites," and also talk with your regular business associates. While this could be an exciting adventure, you'll want to make sure you do it right the first time.

In the meantime, consider the following tips, which offer some of the most important best practices to keep in mind when going mobile:

➡ *Make a light-version of your site.* That's light in terms of size. Make images smaller, optimize the page structure, skip some videos, cut some ads, etc. Websites exceeding one megabyte per page are not easy to download over any wireless connections. Don't make the pages too small either—you want to have some information to offer people.

➡ *Don't skimp on the content.* Having a light site doesn't mean you should leave out content. Some service providers think that mobile users don't need all that content, but that's the wrong approach. You will most like annoy your affluent shoppers if you put one tenth of your content or shortened versions of articles on your mobile site.

➡ *Take it easy with the ads.* While it may be tempting to put ads on your mobile web pages, keep in mind that less is more. Small, relevant

CLICK TIP

Want to see what your site will like before you make it mobile-device friendly? Then check out Skweezer.com (skweezer.com). Simply enter your website's URL, and it will display your website in a mobile-friendly version by removing large images, CSS styles, and page elements that will not display properly. Look at this as a template, or starting point for making a mobile profile for your site.

advertisements are acceptable and might even welcome, but simply posting the current web situation to the mobile side is unacceptable. Also, remember that even a relatively small ad takes up a huge portion of the small mobile screen, so keep things small.

➡ *Don't use Java.* Having Java applets perform any critical function effectively block out all mobile users.

➡ *Make the redirection to the mobile site automatic.* This is one of the most important points. If done right, it does not conflict with the point below on being able to access the full site.

➡ *Allow access to the full site.* Some people may not want to visit only the mobile-optimized site from their device; they would prefer to have access to the full one. It's wrong to force a user to access only the mobile version. This is even more so if you break the other rules. It should, therefore, be possible to easily access the full standard site via a link from the mobile site. Google does this well by putting a link in their mobile version that allows you to access the regular version. Many others have still not gotten there, though it's an exceedingly simple thing to do.

Chapter 8

Search Engine Optimization and Other Marketing Tactics

*T*his chapter will cover some of the most common forms of online marketing today, including search engine optimization, search engine marketing, comparison shopping sites, online display advertising, and affiliate marketing programs, among other tactics. In order to be a successful online boutique owner today, you'll have to be familiar with some, if not all, of these techniques. One more point: While you can set up your online boutique in a week, it takes a bit more time to master these techniques.

Search Engine Optimization Is Essential for Your Online Boutique

Search engine optimization involves getting your site listed with major search engines such as Google (google.com) and Yahoo! (yahoo.com), and then working to constantly maintain and improve your ranking/positioning with each search engine so your site is easy to find and receives top placement.

"Without some type of search engine optimization, the chances of anyone finding your site online are slim to none," says PoshTots.com's Edmunds. "Search engine marketing can provide an effective method for driving highly targeted visitors to your website. Visitors from search engines have voluntarily clicked on your site over your competitors. As a result, they are more likely to explore your offerings."

Registration

The first step is to register your website with the major search engines. This can be done, one at a time, by manually visiting each search engine and completing a new website recommendation form. The process is time consuming and often confusing. An alternative is to pay a third-party submission service to register your site with hundreds of the popular search engines simultaneously.

In addition to accepting submissions from website operators, many search engines and web directories use automated "spiders" or "crawlers" to continuously search the web and gather details about new websites (and updates to existing sites) to list. How these automatic listings are gathered, cataloged, and categorized is based in large part on how your website uses meta tags and keywords throughout the site.

Meta Tags

Meta tags have three parts—the title of your site, a description, and a list of keywords. The information you provide (by incorporating it into your site's HTML programming) is used to categorize your site's content appropriately. In addition to the site's description, title, and list of relevant keywords within the HTML programming of your site, you'll need to incorporate a text-based description of your site (which again uses keywords to describe your site's content.)

The more well-thought-out and comprehensive your meta tags are, the more traffic you'll ultimately generate to your site once it gets added to a search engine. Experts say the description should be a sentence or two describing the content of the web page, using the main keywords and key phrases on this

CLICK TIP

Want to learn more about how to use meta tags? Check out the following link: searchenginewatch.com/showPage.html?page=2167931.

page. If you include keywords that aren't used on the web page, you could hurt yourself. In addition, the maximum number of characters should be about 255.

If your e-commerce turnkey solution doesn't automatically incorporate meta tags into your website, there are many free online tools that allow you to create them and appropriate HTML programming. You then cut-and-paste these lines of programming into your site with ease. No programming knowledge is required. To find these tools, do a simple search of the phrase "meta tag creation."

High Rankings

After your site gets listed with a search engine and appears when searches are conducted by surfers, you then must keep your listing up-to-date and take whatever steps are possible to maintain and improve your listing.

Meta tags can help you score high rankings, but perhaps the best way to score high in search engines is to have good, solid content, especially with regard to the terms that you want to be found for. Experts say it is also important to continually add new content to your site.

Good page titles are extremely helpful. A good page title usually includes five to eight words per page, and does not include filler words such as the, and, etc. Remember: A page title will appear hyperlinked on the search engines when your page is found, so entice searchers to click on the title by making it a bit provocative by using some descriptive keywords along with your business name. The words people are most likely to search on should appear first in the title (called "keyword prominence").

CLICK TIP

Want to know where you rank on the search engines? Software such as WebTrends Inc.'s WebPosition (webposition.com) allows you to check your current search engine ranking and compare your web pages against your top keyword competitors.

Other tips: Make sure your keywords are in your page headline and subheads. Make sure keywords are in the first paragraph of your body text. Use keywords in hyperlinks. Make your navigation system search engine friendly. Develop several pages focused on particular keywords.

SEO can be a time-consuming process you do yourself, or you can hire a SEO expert to handle it on your behalf, which will probably generate better results faster.

If you want or need to have a listing for your site appear on the search engines quickly (as in within hours, not weeks), seriously consider using paid search engine marketing programs to supplement your free listings. We'll discuss these programs below.

Search Engine Marketing

Many online boutique owners also invest in search engine marketing programs that allow them to pay to place their sites in the top results of search

---

SUBMIT YOUR SITE TO ONLINE DIRECTORIES

Try submitting your site to online directories, because listings in these directories help search engines such as Google find, index, and rank your site. For starters, be sure to list your site for free in the Open Directory Project (dmoz.com), which is overseen by thousands of human editors. You also may want to try Yahoo! Directory Submit service (docs.yahoo.com/info/suggest/submit.html). For a $299 annual recurring fee, Yahoo! guarantees that within seven business days a member of Yahoo!'s editorial staff will look at your site and consider it for inclusion in the Yahoo! Directory. Just keep in mind that payment does not automatically guarantee inclusion in the directory or site placement.

---

engines. Basically, every major search engine accepts paid listings—also known as pay-per-click programs—and they are usually marked Sponsored Links on the websites.

These programs allow you to bid on the terms for which you wish to appear. You then agree to pay a certain amount each time someone clicks on your listing. Costs for pay-for-placement start around a nickel a click and go up considerably based on how high you want your site to appear—and competition for keywords has the biggest bearing on costs. For example, a bid on "jewelry" will result in payment of a few bucks a click if you want to get on the first page of results. But if you are promoting say, pearl necklaces, you may be able to get on top paying just a dime a click.

In the Google AdWords program (adwords.google.com), a popular paid placement program, Google sells paid listings that appear above and to the side of its regular results, as well as on its partner sites. Because it may take time for a new site to appear within Google, these advertising opportunities offer a fast way to get listed with the service.

With Google AdWords, the cost of your campaigns really depends on you—how much you're willing to pay and how well you know your audience. It all boils down to knowing your goals and letting Google know what they are. There's a nominal one-time activation fee for Google AdWords of $5, and after that, Google gives the highest position to the advertiser with the highest bid for keywords and the highest click-through rate.

The MSN Search system Microsoft adCenter (adcenter.microsoft.com) is similar to Google AdWords in that all you need is $5 for a one-time signup fee, and the highest position is given to the advertiser with the highest bid for keywords and the highest click-through rate.

Yahoo! Sponsored Search, a service offering from Yahoo! Search Marketing (searchmarketing.yahoo.com), allows you to bid on the keywords for which you wish to appear, and then pay a certain amount each time someone clicks on your listings. For example, if you wanted to appear in the top listings for "clocks," you might agree to pay a maximum of 25 cents per click. If no one agrees to pay more than this, then you would be in the number one spot. If someone later decides to pay 26 cents, then you fall into the number two position. You could then bid 27 cents and move back on top if you wanted to. In other words, the highest bid gets the highest position on Yahoo! Sponsored Search. Yahoo! Sponsored Search displays its listings on its own search results, and MSN, InfoSpace, and other partner sites.

There are two ways to create an account: Through a self-service online channel that requires a $5 deposit (this deposit will be applied to your click-throughs) or through the service Assisted Setup which has a one-time service fee of $199 and includes a custom proposal with suggested keywords, bidding recommendations, and more. Yahoo!'s minimum bid requirement is 10 cents. By carefully selecting targeted terms, you can stretch that money out for one or two months and get quality traffic.

One of the best things about SEM campaigns is that they can be created and launched using a very low budget. At least initially, you'll probably want to experiment with a few different ad variations and keyword lists until you create an ad that has a low cost-per-click and high click-through-rate. Once you've formulated one or more ads that are generating appealing results, you should begin investing hundreds or thousands of dollars into that a campaign. Spending thousands on a campaign that ultimately generates poor results wastes your money and does not generate the traffic to your site that you want and need.

LOCAL SEARCH

Want local customers to find you? Then try local search engine advertising, which lets you target ads to a specific state, city, or even neighborhood. A growing number of small businesses are using local search. Like other search engine advertising, the local variety lets you track your account closely to find out which keywords are most successful at drawing customers and how much you're spending each day. As you can imagine, the major search engine companies offer local search options. To sign up with Yahoo! Search Marketing, for example, go to searchmarketing.Yahoo.com/local. To sign up with Google, go to adwords.google.com/select, and to sign up with MSN, go to advertising.msn.com. In general, all of the programs follow a pay-per-click model.

Although there are myriad choices out there and the concepts may seem confusing, many online boutiques swear by paid search programs. As long as you plan your campaigns carefully, budget properly, and read the fine print, they can really help you improve your reach. "When it comes to advertising quickly and inexpensively, you can't beat pay-per-click programs," says ShopAdorbella.com's Spiegelhalter. "However, I have found that you have to be very careful with it though. If you don't, you can easily end up wasting a lot of money.

Speigelhalter says that if this is the way you decide to go, "I suggest setting a limit and trying different strategies. Also remember: Google, Yahoo!, and MSN aren't the only PPCs out there. There are also comparison-shopping sites that allow people to see the pictures of your items before they click on them."

Comparison Shopping Sites

Attracting qualified traffic, people who are already interested in buying your product or service, is fundamental to your success. That's why online boutique owners should know about comparison shopping sites—also known as "shopping bots." Shopping bots are similar to search engines except that instead of finding information, they're designed to help shoppers find the products or services they're looking for on the internet.

Shopping bot sites list specific product information so shoppers can compare features and prices. This means that shopping bots can be an excellent way for your potential customers to find out exactly what you have to offer—and how to get it. Best of all, shopping bots can be a great place for business owners struggling to stand out in competitive markets to capture the eyeballs of qualified potential customers without spending more than they can afford on the more popular pay-per-click ads like those from Google AdWords.

Though shopping bot sites differ slightly from each other, registering your site and products with most of them is usually pretty easy. In terms of costs, some work on a pay-per-click basis, while other expect a commission on the sale and sometimes a listing fee. Which sites are the leaders? Try AOL Shopping (shopping.aol.com), BizRate (bizrate.com), Google Product Search (google.com/products), NexTag (nextag.com), PriceGrabber (pricegrabber.com), Shopping.com (shopping.com), Shopzilla.com (shopzilla.com), and Yahoo! Shopping (shopping.yahoo.com).

The drawback with these sites, however, is that the potential customer is looking for the lowest price possible. If you're not offering it, they'll simply shop elsewhere. If the products you're selling have a high profit margin, or you're willing to compete with countless other online merchants based mainly on price, price comparison websites can be an extremely viable sales tool.

This type of service also benefits merchants that focus on providing top-notch customer service because the majority of these comparison-shopping sites display customer ratings or rankings. A savvy web surfer/shopper knows to visit an online merchant that has the lowest price and the best customer feedback, all of which is displayed when they use a comparison-shopping site.

Other Linking Strategies

SEO, SEM, and comparison-shopping sites are key ways to get online shoppers to link to your online boutique, but there are additional linking strategies as well. For example, PoshTots.com's Edmunds finds complementary websites and requests a reciprocal link to her site. "Try to partner with other online sites in your same market to see if they will trade links with you," she says. "This will create brand awareness and will not cost anything." But here's a warning: Put the links to other sites on an out-of-the-way page on your site, so you don't send people to another site after working so hard to get them to yours.

You also may want to write articles in your area of expertise and distribute them to editors as free content for their e-mail newsletters or on their websites. For example, if you are an expert on pearl jewelry, you can write an article for a jewelry publication that includes tips on how to choose the best pearl necklaces to buy or sell. Just ask that a link to your website and/or a description of your site be included with the article.

Another key way to draw attention to your online boutique is to use public relations tactics such as releasing press releases to web-based periodicals in your industry or to press release websites. Some leading PR websites include 24-7 Press Release (24-7pressrelease.com), Marketwire (marketwire.com), PRBuzz.com (prbuzz.com), and PRWeb (prweb.com). Placing your online boutique's URL in online copies of your press release also increases link popularity.

In general, SEO and linking strategies can be a great, inexpensive way to get the word out about your online boutique. "Advertising is very expensive, so if you are on a limited budget, stick with marketing tactics such as submitting articles online, link exchanging, search engine optimization, and word-of-mouth campaigns," says PurePearl.com's Raab.

Another inexpensive tactic? According to Raab, it involves building buzz for your online boutique by telling your entire network about your launch. "One of the most important things about running an online business is networking," she says. "I cannot stress it enough. Networking is the most inexpensive key to marketing."

Raab also says the best advice she can give about marketing is to look at it as a long-term investment. "Marketing is something that is done over time," she says. "It is a buildup of credibility and exposure."

> ### CLICK TIP
>
> Advertise your online boutique on a blog. There are a number of blogs that will let you advertise inexpensively. You just need to be careful that you aren't choosing a blog that no one reads (More on blogs in Chapter 9).

Online Display Advertising

Another tactic you may want to use to get visitors to your online boutique is online display advertising, which allows you to purchase ad space on other websites that might appeal to your target audience. Your ads can incorporate text, graphics, animation, sound, and even video to convey your marketing message. Unlike traditional print ads, however, someone who sees your online display ad can simply click on the ad and be transferred to your website in seconds in order to gather more information or make a purchase.

Running online display ads on popular websites costs significantly more than using SEM ads. What your ad says and the visual elements used to convey the message (the overall look of the ad) are equally important. Thus, in addition to spending more to display your ads, you'll probably want to hire a professional advertising agency or graphic artist to design the ads themselves to insure they look professional and are visually appealing.

Depending on where you want your online display ads to appear, size requirements, ad content specifications, and how much you pay will vary dramatically. In addition to choosing appropriate websites to advertise on, you'll need to select the exact placement of your ad on each website's page. Online real estate has value, based on the potential number of people who will be seeing the ad, and the physical size of the ad (which is measured in pixels).

In general, the more people who might be seeing your ad, the higher the ad rates will be. Depending on the website, however, you may have to pay based on overall impressions (the number of people who simply see your ad), or you may only be responsible for paying a predetermined fee only when people click on your ad. Another alternative is to pay a commission when a website referral results in a sale. The payment terms are typically created by the individual website.

The best way to find websites to advertise on is to put yourself in your target customer's shoes and begin surfing the web in search of sites that offer content that's appealing. Next, determine if those sites accept display advertising, and request advertising information if they do. Sites that accept display ads typically have a link on the home page that says "Advertise Here" or "Advertising Information."

Affiliate Programs

Want to generate cash, now, from your online boutique? Try an affiliate marketing program. From Amazon to OfficeMax, leading online retailers are eager to pay you for driving sales their way. How? By putting their link—such as a banner or text—on your site.

For every click-through that results in a sale, you earn a commission, anywhere from 1 to 10 percent for multichannel retailers or 30 to 50 percent in the software sector.

In some cases, you can get commission on all sales that take place up to ten days after you send someone to a site. For example, if a customer visits your site and clicks on the leading online company's banner ad and doesn't buy anything right away but purchases something a few days later, you still get credit for the sale.

In some cases, you are compensated even if the visitor doesn't buy anything. You're paid for just for having driven traffic to the merchant's site. This is not as popular as the former programs, however. The affiliate's reward varies from merchant to merchant and program to program, depending on the terms of the merchant's offer.

There are many independent, third-party affiliate program agencies that will help you create and manage your program. Using any search engine, enter the search phrase, "Affiliate Marketing" or "Affiliate Program." LinkShare (link share.com) continues to be an industry leader when it comes to administering an affiliate program. Other companies include Associate Programs (associate programs.com), Click Booth (clickbooth.com), Commission Junction (cju.cj.com), and Commission Soup (commissionsoup.com).

Supposedly, the idea for affiliate programs—where big merchants enlist small sites as a de facto sales force—got its start when a woman talking with Amazon.com founder Jeff Bezos at a cocktail party in 1996 asked how she might sell books about divorce on her website. Bezos noodled the idea, and a lightbulb went on. He realized the opportunities for both to benefit were great, and the upshot was the launch of Amazon's affiliate program, one of the industry's most successful.

The primary appeal of affiliate marketing is the fact that it is always tied to performance. Marketers are not paying for relationships or placements

---

CLICK TIP

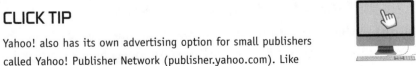

Yahoo! also has its own advertising option for small publishers called Yahoo! Publisher Network (publisher.yahoo.com). Like Google's service, Yahoo!'s self-serve product displays text ads deemed relevant to the content of specific web pages. Advertisers pay only when a reader clicks on their ad. MSN may also start a service as well.

CLICK TIP

The information and message communicated in all of your advertising, marketing, public relations, and promotional efforts should always be consistent with the content on your site and be targeted specifically to the audience to which you're trying to appeal.

that don't work. It is not without risk, nor is it always the most cost-effective in the long term but dollar for dollar, it is usually a good investment.

How big is affiliate marketing? Although it's not as big a part of their overall sales and marketing program as paid search or e-mail, affiliate marketing is an effective strategy to build broader brand awareness and drive motivated buyers to business-to-consumer e-commerce sites, say web retailers participating in the latest *Internet Retailer* (internetretailer.com) survey.

Most web retailers have already made a multiyear investment in affiliate marketing and count on a network of several thousand affiliates to drive visitor traffic, according to the magazine's survey. For instance, 43.2 percent of web merchants taking part in the survey indicate that their affiliate marketing program is at least four years old, compared with 23.2 percent who say they've had a program in place for two to three years, and 10.5 percent with programs only about a year old.

For you, getting a share is simple. You put up a few links on your online boutique (to any of the thousands of e-tailers that offer commissions to affiliates) and as surfers click from your site into your affiliated site, you earn money. All this sounds so new, but think about it. Basically, you're getting paid for leads, a practice as old as selling and one that makes sense for everyone involved.

Google AdSense Makes Sense

Recently, one of the most significant changes in affiliate marketing has been the emergence of Google's AdSense. AdSense (google.com/adsense) allows anyone who publishes online content to display text-based Google AdWords on their website with a simple cut-and-paste format and receive a share of the pay-per-click payment. AdSense ads are similar to the AdWords ads you see on the right-hand side at Google.

SEEING IS BELIEVING

Visual recognition and search company Riya (riya.com) has applied its matching technology to a new fashion shopping site called Like.com (like.com). The idea is that, when a shopper finds a fashion item he or she likes—a particular handbag or pair of shoes, for example—the search engine finds related products by examining the actual image. To get matches, users can do a keyword search, browse products, or even browse items worn by celebrities.

Riya's technology works by studying one image and finding others that match it. Online boutique owners can add their merchandise to Like.com simply by adding item images, or they can work with their affiliate networks to get listed. E-tailers are charged for Like.com's service by the click, but a few merchants use a cost-per-acquisition model.

There are many pluses to using AdSense. For example, proponents say AdSense is simple and free to join, you don't have to use different codes for various affiliate programs, and you can concentrate on providing good content because Google does the work of finding the best ads for your pages from 100,000 AdWords advertisers.

The payment you receive per click depends on how much advertisers are paying per click to advertise using Google's AdWords service. Advertisers can pay as little as 5 cents per click and $10 or $12 in profitable niches, perhaps even more. You earn a share of that.

A key reason for the success of AdSense is its revenue model: It is a cost-per-click model vs. a cost-per-action or cost-per-sale model. In other words, for affiliates to get paid, visitors to a site just have to complete their click instead of having to complete a transaction.

Chapter 9

E-Mail Marketing and Other Advertising Tactics

*F*or many online boutique owners, e-mail is a great tool for building traffic, because it gets results. Customized e-mail can generate response rates upwards of 6 percent—sometimes as high as 30 percent.

Many online boutique owners use e-mail to create a relationship with their current customers—or prospects. A great way to start an e-mail list is to ask your visitors or customers to sign up and permit a company to send messages to them.

What should be included in the content of an e-mail message? Many boutique owners send offers, coupon specials, and product updates to their list of customers and site visitors who have given them permission to contact them. Personalizing the subject line and the message may increase your results, as well.

While it's a big commitment in time, publishing a monthly e-mail newsletter is one of the very best ways to keep in touch with your customers, generate trust, develop brand awareness, and build future business. E-letters can contain industry news, as well as news about new products or special offers you want to promote. In general, it helps you collect e-mail addresses from those who visit your site and make a purchase—or who aren't yet ready

E-MAIL-BASED LOYALTY PROGRAMS

Many online boutique owners use e-mail as the basis for loyalty programs. Acquiring customers isn't as easy as it used to be—so if you have regular customers, it is wise to do something to keep them coming back for more. There are numerous such programs out there. For example, you could something as simple as offering customers the ability to earn gifts—such as T-shirts emblazoned with your logo—if they buy enough merchandise on your site. Or you could go with the most popular option, a frequent-buyer or points program. This choice gives customers the opportunity to receive discounts or points toward the purchase of merchandise by buying products on your site. The more your customers spend—the more times they come back to your site—the bigger the discounts or the more points they receive.

To communicate with customers, you could use e-mail. For example, you could promote the program through your monthly e-newsletter and then send special e-mail messages to members, explaining the gifts they could receive at their point level. Members could also be sent messages about special members-only sales.

Best practices related to online loyalty program include speaking to shoppers' uniqueness, not requiring the user to jump through hoops to participate, and providing a simple reward structure and clear reward and value for information given.

to make a purchase. Ask for an e-mail address and first name so you can personalize the newsletter.

Following the Law

The best way to get people to respond to e-mail is to follow the law. In 2004, Controlling the Assault of Non-Solicited Pornography and Marketing Act (the CAN-SPAM Act of 2003) was signed into law. The law requires *commercial* e-mail messages to be *labeled* and to include *opt-out* instructions as well as the sender's physical address. It also prohibits the use of deceptive *subject lines* and false *headers*.

A good way to get folks to opt-in to your e-mail list—which, of course, they will have the option of opting-out of—is to offer a free monthly e-mail newsletter, which we discussed above.

Content is wide open, but effective newsletters usually mix news about trends in your field with tips and updates on sales or special pricing. Whatever you do, keep it short. Probably 600 words is the maximum length. Another key: Include hyperlinks so that interested readers can, with a single mouse click, go directly to your site and find out more about a topic of interest.

CLICK TIP

Want to learn more about CAN-SPAM? Check out the following link at the Federal Trade Commission's website: ftc.gov/bcp/conline/pubs/buspubs/canspam.shtm.

CLICK TIP

Keep in mind that there are targeted e-mail lists consisting of people who have agreed to receive commercial e-mail messages that you can rent. In general, these lists cost $40 to $400 per thousand or 4-cents to 40-cents per name.

One good idea is to do a smaller e-mail test first to determine the quality of the list. You'll probably want to find an e-mail list broker to help you with this project—you'll save money, sanity, and get experienced help for no additional cost.

Using an ESP

Maintaining an e-mail list can be time-consuming, so a solution to common mailing hassles is to use an e-mail service provider. When choosing an ESP, the ESP should be an expert on all things e-mail and should share this information proactively to improve the effectiveness of your e-mail. It should also understand and be able to advise you on legal issues from a best practice perspective in all the markets where you send e-mail messages—including other countries. It should offer support when needed by you, not when it is convenient for it, and it should be able to help you implement advanced tools such as dynamic content and web analytics into your e-mail campaigns. Finally, it should offer reports regularly that show how a particular campaign is performing for you.

Three good choices for online boutique owners just starting out include: Constant Contact (constantcontact.com), ExactTarget (exattarget.com), and Topica (topica.com). These services maintain mailing lists and on your schedule, send out the mailings you provide.

A lot of the grunt work involved in e-mailings is handled by these services, which leaves you free to focus on the fun part: your message. Keep it simple, keep it sharp, and always use e-mail to drive traffic to your site. Don't make the big mistake of trying to cram your website's entire message into every e-mail. Nobody has the patience for that. E-mail should stick to headline news, with the full story residing on your website.

List Success

There's no reason to guess at whether your list is succeeding. Just track site traffic for a few days before a mailing and a few days afterwards. Effective e-mail ought to produce a sharp upward spike in visitors. How big a spike hinges on your usual traffic, the size of your list, and your personal goals. A good target, though, is a 6 percent response rate.

If you don't see an increase in traffic, take a hard look at what you're mailing. Is it succinct? Focused? Does it encourage readers to click through for more information? If not, odds are you need to hone your message to encourage recipients to click through.

CLICK TIP

Want to use e-mail in a whole new way? Then buy a text ad in an e-mail newsletter—not yours but someone else's. Some of the best buys are small text ads in e-mail newsletters targeted at audiences likely to be interested in your products or services. Or, consider exchanging e-mail newsletter ads with complementary businesses to reach new audiences. Just be sure that your partners are careful where they get their mailing list or you could be in trouble with the CAN-SPAM Act.

Another possible reason for less-than-desirable results is that your mailing list is bad. Send a vegan mailing to a list of self-proclaimed steak lovers, and you're knocking on the wrong door. The best way to build a targeted mailing list is to make it simple for site visitors to sign up to receive your e-mails. By doing that, they show they are interested in your message—enough to indicate they want to hear more from you. Those are the folks who should be stimulated by your e-mail newsletter to click through for more info, at least sometimes. Keep working on both your newsletter and your list, and it will happen for you, too.

CLICK TIP

The internet offers thousands of very targeted e-mail-based discussion lists, online forums, blogs, and usenet newsgroups made up of people with very specialized interests. Use Google Groups to find appropriate sources (groups.google.com). Don't bother with newsgroups consisting of pure spam. Instead, find groups where a serious dialog is taking place. Also, be sure not to use aggressive marketing or overtly plug your online boutique. Rather, add to the discussion in a helpful way and let the signature at the end of your e-mail message do your marketing for you. People will gradually get to know and trust you, visit your site, and do business with you.

BEST PRACTICES FOR SUCCESSFUL DELIVERY OF E-MAIL MARKETING COMMUNICATIONS

In its report "E-mail Delivery Best Practices for Marketers and List Owners," the Direct Marketing Association (the-dma.org) offers some practical advice for marketers about how to be more successful at reaching current and potential customers or donors through focused e-mail messages.

The best practices are intended to improve the likelihood of permission-based e-mail being delivered to the inbox and read by the intended recipient. Some of the broad recommendations from the e-mail best practices include suggestions that e-mail marketers should:

➡ Encourage customers and prospects to add your legitimate sending address to their personal approved list/address book and provide up-front instructions on how to do so in registration pages. Benefits vary by mailbox provider, but may include special icon designation and full image content/link rendering. Being an approved sender yields higher response rates and generates fewer complaints and blocking issues.

➡ Carefully consider the content and presentation of marketing messages. Recipients are increasingly labeling any e-mail communication that is not relevant or looks suspicious as spam. In addition, you should create messages that strike a balance between images and system text, because many mailbox providers now routinely "hide" images in default settings.

➡ Follow established protocols such as authentication criteria to ensure that e-mail messages pass muster with mailbox providers. A growing number of ISPs use spam-filtering software to eliminate spam. This technology uses algorithms to determine whether incoming messages qualify as junk e-mail and filters them out before they get to an end-user's inbox. In addition, register for all mailbox provider feedback loops. In general, you should aim to keep complaint rates (total complaints divided by total delivered e-mail) below 0.1 percent to avoid temporary or long-term blocks.

BEST PRACTICES FOR SUCCESSFUL DELIVERY OF E-MAIL MARKETING COMMUNICATIONS, CONTINUED

➡ Adopt good list hygiene and monitoring practices to help facilitate message delivery. Monitoring campaign delivery, open and click-through rates, is essential because a low open rate or high bounce rate may indicate a delivery issue.

➡ Educate consumers and other stakeholders about antispam tools, technologies, laws, and industry programs developed to separate legitimate communications from fraudulent messaging.

Traditional Media

For some online boutique owners, traditional media—used in conjunction with e-mail, search, and other digital marketing tools—is very effective. For example, try promoting your online boutique through display or classified ads you purchase in trade journals, newspapers, Yellow Pages, etc.

But be sure to include your URL in any advertising. In fact, view your website as an information adjunct to the ad. Use a two-step approach: First, capture readers' attention with the ad, and second, refer them to a URL where they can obtain more information and perhaps place an order.

Also, look carefully at small display or classified ads in the back of narrowly targeted magazines or trade periodicals. Sometimes these ads are more targeted, more effective, and less expensive than online advertising.

In addition, consider other traditional media to drive people to your site. Direct mail, classifieds, postcards, and TV can be used to promote websites, especially in a local market.

CLICK TIP

Do you include your URL on your stationery, cards, and any other literature? This no-brainer is sometimes overlooked. Make sure that all reprints of cards, stationery, brochures, and literature contain your company's URL. And see that your printer gets the URL syntax correct. In print, leave off the "www." part and include only the domain.com portion.

FIVE TIPS ON EFFECTIVE NEWS RELEASES

Writing news releases may not be second nature for online boutique owners. Here are some tips:

1. *Make sure your release is newsworthy.* Good topics include the announcement of a major new client or community service performed by your company.

2. *Create news and put out a press release about it.* Speak at a seminar, for example, or provide expert comment on developing news events.

3. *Get your releases to the right people.* Find out whom at your radio and TV stations and newspaper will be the most interested in your news.

4. *Capture editors' attention by putting the news in the first paragraph.* Then add the necessary details.

5. *Make your releases look crisp and professional; that means no smudgy type.* Include the name and phone number of a contact person, and answer media queries promptly.

Make sure to take advantage of any public relations opportunities. Send press releases out to trade reporters or local news organizations. Many of these organizations love to write about small, successful businesses—especially those selling interesting luxury items. "Think public relations," says Tonic Home's Linda Hayes. "Free media is always the way to go. Market your story to reporters and start contacting bloggers in your industry."

But there is more to it then just randomly calling reporters in your industry. Here are some tips for getting press for your online boutique:

➡ *Do your homework.* Target television programs, cable programs, newspapers, and trade magazines, among other media vehicles, that fit with your design style.

➡ *Create a professional-looking press kit.* Approach this as you would applying for a job. You create a cover letter addressed to a person (find this person on the masthead of the magazine or the credits of a TV show.)

Add a few pictures of your product, a bio page and your contact information, and those are the basics. For a really professional looking press kit, you may have to use a freelancer.

➡ *Tell a story.* This is a key task. How do you do this? By sharing a little bit about yourself on your bio page. What is your design inspiration?

PAPER-BASED SALES

After opening their online boutique, many entrepreneurs expand their reach by adding a catalog to the mix. Why? Because the tried-and-true catalog sent streaming through the mail along with all those bills, letters, and notices is still the top-rated method of garnering customers—and, of course, sales. What's more, being a multi-merchant can be good for your business.

Research conducted by comScore Networks for the U.S. Postal Service found that a business doubles its chances of making an online sale by mailing a catalog.

Other findings from "The Multi-Channel Catalog Study" include:

➡ Catalog recipients account for 22 percent of traffic to a catalog company's website and 37 percent of its e-commerce dollars.

➡ Catalog recipients make 16 percent more visits to that company's website than those who do not receive a catalog.

➡ Catalog recipients view 22 percent more pages and spend 15 percent more time at the website than those who do not receive a catalog.

➡ On average, the total amount spent on a website by a catalog recipient is $39, more than twice the $18 spent by non-catalog consumers.

Catalogs also work well as a channel for e-tailers because they can easily leverage the website's marketing, creative, infrastructure, and fulfillment systems and repurpose them for a catalog.

Why did you start an online boutique? Give them a quick one or two lines about your marketing philosophy or about the merchandise you sell.

➡ *Be timely.* Remember that TV shows and magazines are working about three months in advance of airing or print. Newspapers (don't forget local publications) have a shorter lead time. But don't send something talking about holiday gift guides in November. They have set these issues months before.

➡ *Be patient.* Jewelry, for example, is very competitive. Take the time to evolve your business image and learn to edit your descriptions (and your designs!). Learn about the industry and discover your niche. Don't worry if you aren't in the black yet. It takes time to grow a healthy business. Keep your goals realistic while still having the stretch goals of world domination.

➡ *Be professional.* Respond in a timely manner to a query about your shop, keep the casual chatter with a reporter to a minimum, and remember, relationships are everything.

Chapter 10

Social Media Marketing and Online Boutiques

*I*nternet marketing has given birth to social media marketing, and it would be wise for online boutique owners to take notice. Social media marketing is a form of internet marketing that seeks to achieve branding and marketing communication goals through participation in various social media networks such as MySpace (myspace.com), Facebook (facebook.com), and YouTube (youtube.com), as well as through social web applications such as reddit (reddit.com), Digg (digg.com), Stumbleupon (stumbleupon.com), Flickr (flickr.com), iLike (ilike.com), Wikipedia (wiki pedia.com), Squidoo (squidoo.com), and Twitter (twitter.com). It also includes working within 3D virtual worlds such as Second Life (secondlife .com), ActiveWorlds (activeworlds.com), Moove (moove.com), and There.com (there.com).

Social media marketing is part of the umbrella term Web 2.0, a trend in web technology and web design, where a second generation of web-based communities and hosted services such as social-networking sites, wikis, blogs, and folksonomies facilitate creativity, collaboration, and sharing among users. The central theme of these sites is user-generated content with the social aspects of allowing users to set up social communities, invite friends, and share common interests. Social media marketing also refers to the blogs, wikis, podcasts, or RSS feeds that online boutique owners use on their websites or in other communications with customers and suppliers.

In general, the goals of each social media marketing program or campaign differs for every business or organization, but most involve some form of building an idea or brand awareness, increasing visibility, encouraging brand feedback and dialogue, as well as selling a product or service.

CLICK TIP

As you wade through the social media waters, you'll probably hear the term "tag" a lot. According to Wikipedia, "a tag is a (relevant) keyword or term associated with or assigned to a piece of information (a picture, a geographic map, a blog entry, a video clip, etc.), thus describing the item and enabling keyword-based classification and search of information."

Tags are usually chosen informally and personally by the item author/creator or by its consumer/viewers/community. Tags are typically used for resources such as computer files, web pages, digital images, and internet bookmarks, both in social bookmarking services, and in the current generation of web browsers. For this reason, "tagging" has become associated with the Web 2.0 social media buzz. Just an FYI.

What types of social media marketing tools should you use? Read on to find out. Each technique is different, so make sure to experiment with the ones that seem the most interesting and economically feasible for you.

Social Networking Sites on the Rise

Think social networking sites are just for teens and tweens who post party photos and lists of favorite bands? Think again. A new generation is flocking to internet-based social networking sites and they may well be the adult consumers most likely to make a luxury purchase.

Over 40 percent of luxury consumers visited a social networking site, such as Facebook, YouTube, or MySpace between August and October 2007. This is the most surprising finding of a new survey by Unity Marketing (unitymarketingonline.com) on how luxury consumers are using the internet. Unity Marketing is a boutique market research firm specializing in consumer insights for marketers and retailers that sell luxury goods and experiences.

The survey was conducted in October 2007 among 1,074 affluent consumers who made at least one luxury purchase in the past three months (average income $150,200 and age 43.6 years) "This study shows the method behind Microsoft's 'madness' in paying $240 million for only 1.6 percent of Facebook. It isn't just kids visiting the social networking sites like Facebook anymore. Even middle-aged affluent consumers are networking online," says Pam Danziger, president of Unity Marketing and author of *Shopping: Why We Love It and How Retailers Can Create the Ultimate Customer Experience*. (Kaplan Publishing, 2006). "Young affluents, those 40 years and under, were the most active social networkers, but even one-third of the over 40 year old consumers reported visiting a social networking site."

The study revealed that when it comes to their favorite websites for shopping, Amazon.com—with its wide range of product offerings—received top billing from luxury consumers. Following Amazon.com in the ranking was eBay (number 2), Nordstrom.com (number 3), Macys.com and Overstock.com (tied for number 4), and Neimanmarcus.com (number 5). A complete list of the websites named in the survey is available by clicking on the Unity Marketing site.

The study also found that over half (52 percent) of consumers of home luxury products and 46 percent of buyers of luxury fashion, fashion accessories, cosmetics, jewelry, and watches used the internet in support of their recent luxury purchases. "The internet has a powerful influence on luxury consumers in terms of their spending. For example, those customers who used the internet for home luxury purchases spent 11 percent more on their homes, while those who used the internet for their personal luxury purchases spent 12.5 percent more on average buying fashion, jewelry, watches, and cosmetic products.

"They used the internet both to research purchases, especially to compare prices and read other customers' reviews, as well as to make purchases. The research also shows that they will visit a retailer's website to 'browse' before they head out to the store. The lesson is that luxury marketers and retailers which offer their customers a website get a significant return on investment in terms of more spending," Danziger says.

When it comes to the features that luxury consumers value most in the internet, the convenience of shopping at home is right at the top of the list, along with having a wide selection of merchandise available online. They also are passionate about the tools that the internet gives them to compare prices and evaluate product features. It saves them time and makes shopping less of a chore.

The many pluses of internet shopping make up for any minor inconveniences, such as shipping and handling charges and delays in receiving the merchandise. Other issues, however, are more of a hindrance to luxury shoppers. Some 35 percent of luxury consumers are very discouraged about using the internet to make purchases because of difficulties in returns and exchanges. And 21 percent are uneasy about making big ticket purchases, for example, kitchen appliances and jewelry, online.

"When asked what features were most important for a luxury shopping site to offer these luxury consumers, they were adamant about three features: in-depth product information and specifications, detailed product pictures, and a flexible return policy. They were far less concerned with company or brand news, lifestyle content, or a store locator," Danziger says.

Travel is the one category where the internet has really penetrated the luxury market. Commenting on the research, Danziger says, "Luxury consumers are maxing out the capabilities of the internet in terms of their luxury travel. Over 90 percent of luxury consumers used the internet in support of their travel planning in the third quarter," she says. "Over 80 percent made travel reservations online and researched travel destinations. More than half (56 percent) visited a website to see what other travelers have to say about their destination."

Danziger adds, "This study shows just how important the internet is as a resource in support of the luxury consumers' lifestyle. Its value as a shopping venue is without question, but for marketers and retailers its role in influencing and informing the shopper cannot be ignored. So when making investment decisions pertaining to the internet, marketers need to carefully measure its power in advertising, promoting, and building the company's brand and not just take into account the cash flow resulting directly from internet purchases."

CLICK TIP

Want to learn more about how luxury consumers use the internet? Then check out unitymarketingonline.com/cms_luxury/luxury/luxury3/Luxury_Tracking_3Q2007.php to learn more about its study of the "Luxury Consumers and Their Use of the Internet."

Blogging for Business

A great way to get links to your site is to start a blog and post it on your online boutique. A blog is a web log that is updated regularly—sometimes daily, sometimes a few times a week. It contains information related to a specific topic. In some cases blogs are daily diaries about people's personal lives, political views, or even as social commentaries. Blogs can be shaped into whatever you, the author, want them to be.

Blogs can be created in-house or with a blogging software. Leading blogging software providers include Blogger (blogger.com), TypePad (typepad.com), and Wordpress (wordpress.com).

There are a lot of reasons why blogging is such a great thing for your online boutique business. Below are the five most important reasons why a blog will definitely help your online boutique and increase your sales.

1. *It helps build a relationship with customers.* Blogs allow you to create content and contact, and that is what your customers crave more than

anything. Blogging enables you to build a more personal relationship with your customer. By offering your opinions on issues, you are essentially letting readers know that there is actually a real person behind your website and who that person is. By enabling visitors to comment on your blog entries, you automatically create a one-to-one relationship and a fun way to keep people coming back. People have the tendency to crave interesting content: they like to look in on people's lives. Keeping them entertained with pictures and stories is a great way to keep them interested in you and your merchandise.

2. *Search engines love blogs.* Search engines crave content, especially new and updated content. While providing content, not to mention fresh content, may be one of the toughest chores of anyone who maintains a website, it is the most important job when it comes to generating traffic. Blogs, by their very nature, are all about content. In a commercial environment every blog entry is fresh content. Get in the habit of writing two, three, even four entries a week and you'll build a real love affair with your search engines. Everyone knows you need new content to give visitors a reason to come back; blogging just makes the task so much easier.

3. *Targeted keywords bring you traffic.* By using targeted keywords in your entry titles, you can make your web log a traffic magnet. Enough said.

4. *You can show your passion.* One of the most important things to remember when starting a blog is to make sure to write what interests you and what you know. But also remember that you can blog about almost anything. If you don't want your blog to be about you, you don't have to write about yourself. You can write strictly about your product, for example, or making it, and drive in visitors that are interested only in this. You can also write about your creative process, your spiritual life, or anything that inspires you. The most important points are to be creative, colorful, and interesting. That keeps your visitors coming back for more.

5. *It helps to build a community.* You can build a great community of like-minded people around your blog. Start by finding blogs that are on the same theme as yours and comment on their entries, leaving your

UPGRADING YOUR BLOG

It is pretty easy to set up a blog (though continuing to write for it is definitely not so easy). However, you can also upgrade the effectiveness of your blog by adding videos (as you would on your website), publicizing it with free services such as Pingoat (pingoat.com), burning an RSS feed with FeedBurner (feedburner.com), or inserting slide shows with Slide (slide.com).

Pingoat is a service that pings or notifies a number of services that keep track of blogs and publish them. By pinging, you let the services know that your blog has been updated, so, they crawl and index your site, publishing your blog contents, thus increasing your blog's popularity.

FeedBurner is a leading provider of media distribution and audience engagement services for blogs and RSS feeds. Its web-based tools help bloggers, podcasters, and commercial publishers promote, deliver, and profit from their content on the web. FeedBurner can help publicize your content and make it easy for people to subscribe; optimize distribution so that your content is properly formatted for all of the major directories and can be consumed by subscribers wherever they are; and a learn how many subscribers you have, where they're coming from, and what they like best. For even more exposure, you can join the FeedBurner Ad network. Why not reward yourself for your effort?

Slide, the largest personal media network in the world, reaches 144 million unique global viewers each month and more than 30 percent of the U.S. internet audience. Slide's products—including Slideshows, FunWall, and SuperPoke!—are popular on top social networking and blog platforms, including MySpace, Facebook, Bebo, Hi5, Friendster, Tagged, and Blogger. Slide is also the leading developer on Facebook with more than 84 million applications installed and has more active users than any other developer.

web address anywhere you can. With this, you will drive visitors who checked other blogs to your blog. Next, you can register with blog search engines (which you can find via a simple Google search), or try trading some links. A few swapped links to related blogs can definitely boost your traffic.

Try Podcasting

Podcasting is another social technique you may want to include on your online boutique or use in an e-mail campaign to get visitors to your site. A podcast is simply a series of audio files that you make available for others to hear. It is called a podcast because it is usually broadcast on a regular basis like a radio show. Listeners, however, have the convenience of listening to the podcast on their computer or MP3 player, such as an iPod. Another feature of a podcast is that its availability is often announced via RSS feed.

People love podcasts because they are freed from manually checking their favorite audio-enabled websites to download new files. With podcasts, people set their aggregators to download audio files just before they head for work in the morning or whatever activity they do. When they're ready to go, they can take the files with them. But podcast listeners are attracted not only to the mobility factor but also to the ability to have the MP3 already downloaded onto their PC and ready to listen to whenever they are.

CLICK TIP

Want step-by-step course to help you get started with podcasts? Check out the affordable Shoestring Radio and Podcasting course at shoestringradio.com.

Another plus? Audio is easier to produce than text. It's much easier and faster to record an audio newsletter or message than to sit and type something for a blog or website. Podcasts are more personal because people can hear you, your personality comes through, and it seems like you're speaking directly to them. So it's great for building that relationship. It can also distribute your message to listeners in a timely fashion, without concern about spam, filters, or any of that stuff associated with e-mail marketing.

RSS Marketing Feeding Frenzy

A social media tool that many online boutique owners are using more and more is RSS, or Really Simple Syndication. RSS feeds, which automatically

POST A PODCAST ON YOUR SITE

Want to try podcasting on your site? Follow these eight simple steps, and you'll be posting podcasts on your online boutique in no time.

Step 1: Create an audio file using your favorite audio recording software. If you are unfamiliar with audio recording software, you might want to try Audacity (audacity.com).

Step 2: Convert your audio file to MP3 format. MP3 format is the standard format for podcasts. Converting the files ensures that all of your listeners will be able to hear them. If you use Audacity, you can simply export your file to MP3 format. Other audio software should work similarly.

Step 3: Upload your MP3 file to your web server.

Step 4: Create a link to your MP3 file on the web page on which you wish to publish your podcast. Create a link that listeners can click to open your file. Your link will look similar to this: yourwebsite.com/myfirstpodcast.mp3.

Step 5: Write a title and brief description of your podcast above or below the link to the podcast so listeners will know what your podcast is about.

Step 6: Create an RSS feed for your podcast. Your RSS feed will include your podcast title, description, and link. You can create an RSS feed easily by using the free podcast RSS Feed Generator by TD Scripts.

Step 7: Add your podcast RSS feed to your website by uploading your newly created RSS file. This file should be saved and uploaded as an .xml file. It is the file your listeners will use to subscribe to your podcast.

Step 8: Let your website visitors know that you have a new podcast. Provide the link to your podcast RSS feed on your website.

deliver updated digital content to subscribers, are gaining popularity with online boutique owners.

They are particularly well-suited for marketing activities that involve loyal customers checking for updates in fares, prices, availability, and new items, says Charlene Li, a vice president and principal analyst at Forrester Research Inc. in Cambridge, Massachusetts. "Feeds allow customers to simply subscribe to an alert that notifies them when information that meets their criteria is available—and [they] do so without cluttering the inbox," she says.

Some best practices for RSS marketing include:

➡ *Make subscription easy.* RSS is new to many customers, but companies still make the mistake of linking an orange RSS button to an XML page, hoping their customers will figure it out. Develop subscription pages that explain RSS feeds and how to subscribe in plain English.

➡ *Offer relevant content.* This is the key to retaining subscribers. Use a content preferencing page to ensure subscribers get the content they want. Popular e-commerce content includes special offers, new products, and blogs written by merchandisers.

➡ *Measure.* Due to the ease of unsubscribing, per-subscriber analytics are especially important to assess the performance of your RSS program. By judiciously analyzing your customers' interests and making appropriate changes in your content, you can build your active subscriber base.

Adding Reviews to Your Site

Another collaborative social media tool you may want to add to your online boutique is a customer review function. This feature will let you know what your customers think of your products by letting them tell other customers (and you) by posting their comments on your website. What's more, according to the Luxury Institute (luxuryinstitute.com), an independent research institution that focuses solely on the top 10 percent of America's wealthy, 84 percent of consumers earning more than $150,000 annually visit sites where customers review and rate products and services, including restaurants.

> **CLICK TIP**
>
> A great way to get your site known is through setting up a friends network account such as MySpace, where you can quickly tell friends and family about your new merchandise and website. This can work well as your friends may tell their friends, and so on.

SOCIAL MEDIA SPENDING

By 2013, advertisers and marketers are expected to spend more money on so-called conversational media—or online media products such as blogs and podcasts—than on advertising through traditional media, such as print and radio. So says a recent study from the Society for New Communications Research (SNCR), (sncr.org) global nonprofit think tank dedicated to the advanced study of new communications tools, technologies, and emerging modes of communication, and their effect on traditional media, professional communications, business, culture, and society.

An earlier study on social media spending by Prospero (prospero.com) reported that 88 percent of businesses expected to increase social media spending in 2008. Furthermore, when asked about social media return on investment (ROI), 35 percent reported positive ROI and 41 percent said that ROI was unknown. Responses to questions about how web marketers measure ROI reveal that direct sales revenue is not a top measure for determining social media success. Respondents said that total number of site visitors (17 percent) was the most important criterion for assessing social media performance. Total number of page views and number of subscribers/community members (15 percent each) were next, followed closely by length of visit on the site (14 percent).

According to the Prospero study, traffic to social media sites is the most important determiner of ROI (which suggests investment in social media is advertising driven, perhaps more than it should be). On the other hand, brand engagement is the main measure of success for social media spending, although there are no common definition of what "engagement" is.

As plenty of online boutique owners have discovered, online reviews by happy customers carry more weight with other buyers than most other forms of marketing communication. A number of companies offer tools to help you get started. PowerReviews (powerreviews.com) offers an outsourced solution. Bazaarvoice's (bazaarvoice.com) hosted and managed solution monitors reviews and updates them regularly. The Prospero CommunityCM platform (prospero.com) lets you manage online reviews yourself.

E-tailers also gain market share through user-generated product ratings/reviews. That was a key finding of "Retail Marketing: Driving Sales Through Consumer-Created Content" from New York-based Jupiter Research (jupiterresearch.com).The report found that the number of online buyers who cite customer ratings and reviews as the most useful shopping site feature has more than doubled from 2005 to 2006. In addition, survey respondents said user-generated ratings and reviews are now the second most important site feature behind search. Finally, the report found 60 percent of online shoppers provide feedback about a shopping experience and they are more likely to give feedback about a positive experience than a negative one.

Promote Your Online Boutique with Social Bookmarking Sites

Social bookmarking is all the rage these days and it's time to get in on the act. Social bookmarking services allow users to share other pages—such as blogs, articles, videos and other types of website content—around the internet that they find worthwhile. Some of the better places allow users to give reviews, vote on pages, and share pages with friends.

What does this mean for online boutique owners? By getting your pages linked at social bookmarking sites, you'll be building links back to your website. All you need to do is one or all of the following: 1) Create an account and add the pages yourself; 2) provide the links to social bookmarking sites on your pages and prompt visitors to go bookmark your pages; 3) pay someone to add your pages to their accounts.

CLICK TIP

Do you ask your visitors to bookmark your site to make it easier to get to? If not, you should. It seems so simple, but make sure you do it.

Creating an account and adding the pages yourself is a good starting point. You'll get to see firsthand how the social bookmarking place works. However, some places don't want you to add your own sites. Therefore options two and three would be better. Make it your goal to get each page you have socially bookmarked. Whenever you add a new page of content to your website, proceed to follow one of the methods discussed above.

If you use options two or three, how can you get users to bookmark your page? Follow these tips:

- ➡ *Figure out what people like.* Pay special attention to the blogs, websites, and articles that are bookmarked the most and ranked the highest. This will give you an idea of what people like to see.
- ➡ *Offer something interesting.* The blogs and websites that do best in the social bookmarking arena are those that offer entertainment, worthy news, or some sort of draw.
- ➡ *Stick to quality content.* When submitting content to social bookmarking sites, it is essential to stick to submitting quality content. Once you get traffic flowing to your websites and blogs, the sales will follow naturally, especially if you focus on conversion optimization on your site or blog.
- ➡ *Remember that timing is everything.* Articles that get at least 20 votes within the first 10 minutes will rise through the social bookmarking ranks faster than articles that get 20 votes in two days' time.
- ➡ *Don't open several accounts.* Opening several accounts on one social bookmarking site so that you can vote for yourself should be avoided. This will only damage your reputation if you are found to be promoting your own blogs and affiliate marketing programs.

Social bookmarking sites are sprouting up all the time. A quick search will give you a listing of many places to try. Some of the leading ones are: Blinklist (blink list.com), Del.icio.us (del.icio.us), Digg (digg .com), Reddit (reddit.com), Stumbleupon (stumbleupon.com), and Propeller (pro peller.com).

> ## CLICK TIP
>
>
>
> Check out Squidoo .com (squidoo.com). This website lets you create so-called lenses that can contain your articles, photos, and feeds from a blog, reviews, link lists, and more. You can also include ads by Amazon.com or other online shops and will receive a commission on affiliate income.

Using Video

Consider making a video website or adding one to your existing online boutique. There are several great reasons to do so, but the biggest is that when used properly and with professionalism, your video website helps increase your bottom line by building the rapport and superior trust with your customer that simple text cannot duplicate. In addition, there is a social component where it can be passed around and viewed by others.

Video creates that extra sense of professionalism and it is also a great way to keep a customer's attention. These days, people's attention spans seem not to last longer than a few minutes. What's more, as we mentioned when discussing rich media, consumers buying high-value merchandise want to know everything about what they are buying online—and rightly so. Video allows this—and a dialogue with consumers so they can see who you really are and trust you. Also, once you have a video made, you can post it on a video-sharing site such as YouTube (youtube.com) to extend your brand.

There are many tools out there that can help you make a video, so do your research, network, and start taping. But although you can create videos for your online boutique yourself, it is not recommended. You'll probably want to hire a professional who specializes in creating high-quality video for websites. To find one, ask your business network or do a search for internet video or web video online or in your local Yellow Pages. Many companies can manage projects—from simple YouTube-style clips to elaborate productions—from start to finish.

Still, many do people want to participate in their video projects and perhaps reduce costs by doing some of the work themselves. Here are ideas to consider.

➡ *If you already have great video that delivers your message, use it.* Many companies have had a DVD professionally made or had video created for a TV spot. It is easy and affordable to reformat that existing video and use it on the internet.

➡ *Post audio and video from a radio or TV spot that may have already run.* If you have had something professionally produced, you may as well make it available on your online boutique. Just take the audio output from a CD player or other source and put it into the line-in jack on your computer. Use Audacity (audacity.com) or some other audio editing software to capture and manipulate the sound.

➡ *If you have great still photos, consider turning them into a narrated video slideshow*. This can be very effective, at a cost that is far lower than you would pay to shoot and edit new video. Some of the biggest companies in the world use video created solely from still images, and you hardly notice it doesn't show full action. You can pan and zoom on the photos to give them movement.

➡ *Use a great script*. The prettiest images in the world will benefit you but little unless they are presented alongside relevant selling points and a compelling call to action. Think through your presentation. What is it you want the clip to accomplish? Work that out before you start storyboarding and shooting video.

➡ *If you need to get new video shot, hire a professional*. The quality you get from a consumer-grade camcorder just doesn't compare with images delivered via more expensive professional-grade equipment. Also, a professional will be able to use advanced camera techniques to make the video shine.

CLICK TIP

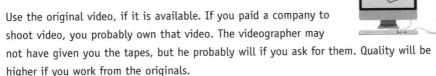

Use the original video, if it is available. If you paid a company to shoot video, you probably own that video. The videographer may not have given you the tapes, but he probably will if you ask for them. Quality will be higher if you work from the originals.

If you can't get the tapes, you can still get reasonable quality by pulling the video from a DVD. Use a good DVD player to output S-Video (also known as separate video) to a quality digital camcorder, then go from the camcorder into a computer for editing. You can do the same with video from a VHS tape, but that quality does not compare with the clear image delivered via DVD.

➡ *Get the video edited.* Again, we recommend using a professional if you want high quality. You can edit video on most newer computers using Microsoft's Windows Movie Maker (microsoft.com) or Apple's I-Movie (apple.com) and get a decent basic clip, but you will need more sophisticated tools if you want to create something truly outstanding.

➡ *Post your clip to YouTube and then embed it into a page on your site.* YouTube makes it very easy to get video onto the internet, and easy to get it into one of your web pages. The quality of clips on YouTube varies greatly. Basically, if you upload decent video, YouTube will deliver a clip of acceptable quality. If you want outstanding quality, then you should get someone who specializes in internet video to format it and post it to your server.

YouTube gives you a potentially huge audience. For most people, the ease of posting and the potentially large audience are important benefits. You will get the most mileage from your clip if you deliver it to the diverse audience found on YouTube, *and* to the targeted audience that visits your website.

NEIMAN MARCUS ON YOUTUBE

Yes, you read that right. A documentary-style video marking Neiman Marcus's 100th anniversary was posted on YouTube in the fall of 2007. The luxury retail chain was celebrating its latest milestone in a series of four-minute video clips featuring Richard Marcus, the company's CEO, and top designers talking about their favorite memories and attributes of the company.

The first video "The Mystique Part 1," was posted on Sept. 9, and had more than 75,000 viewers after only three days.

The posting was part of an effort by YouTube to expand video advertising sales. The first video was featured on YouTube's home page, and then visitors could visit a Neiman Marcus page on You Tube to see the other videos.

Adding Widgets to Your Site

Try widgets to get more people interested in your site for low- or no-cost. Widgets, also called "gadgets", are like mini television screens that contain information such as your brand, logo, or any interesting information pertaining to your brands that can be posted on a website, blog, or desktop. Visitors to your website will see it, download it, and post it on their own blogs or Facebook (facebook.com) pages. Almost immediately, your brand is now in front of thousands of new consumers, who only need to click on the widget to be redirected to your site. A widely distributed widget can increase traffic to your website and boost your search engine rankings.

Widgets are becoming more and more popular. For example, comScore says widget-adorned web pages reached 239 million unique visitors in June 2007, up from 178 million when comScore started tracking widgets in April 2007.

Keep in mind that your widget doesn't have to be fancy to be a success. Building one is relatively easy—a skilled computer programmer can do it in just a few hours. You can also use one of the thousands of widgets readily available on the web. Many of the widgets are customizable; you can add your company name and logo and decide what information will appear on it.

Here's a roundup of some handy web widgets to get your online boutique started on the right foot:

➡ *FormLogix (formlogix.com)*. When you are bootstrapping a web startup, you can't always afford a professional web designer or programmer to help build your site out. Fortunately, FormLogix makes it easy to add anything—such as a contact form, order form, or testimonial form—to your site. Its premade widgets are the fastest way to get started.

CLICK TIP

Try social media site Flickr.com (flickr.com) to let you upload photos and "tag" them. It is a good way to showcase your work if you do not have your own online boutique up yet or to supplement the reach of your website. However, it is not a marketplace. The community guidelines state, "Flickr is for personal use only. If you sell products, services or yourself through your photostream, we will terminate your account."

➡ *Cooqy (cooqy.com).* Cooqy creates free, customizable widgets you can embed in your website, blog, or social networking page, on a site such as MySpace (myspace.com) or Facebook. Using the widgets on eBay pages such as item listings is free if you have fewer than 500 active listings; it's $4.95 per month if you have more than that.

➡ *Shopit (shopit.com).* With this social commerce widget, you get a free online portable store that can be embedded as a widget in blogs and on social networking sites. Yahoo! and eBay Store users can easily import their entire catalogs as well.

➡ *Cartfly (cartfly.com).* Cartfly is similar to Shopit. You can customize your portable online boutique to fit your business's look and style. Accounts are free to set up but include a 3 percent transaction fee. The emphasis is on a simple interface with a fast setup that will help you get your store out and about on the web in no time.

Looking for a specific widget? Go to widget directories Google Gadgets (google.com/webmasters/gadgets) or Widgetbox (widgetbox.com) for searchable

EXPERIMENTING IN VIRTUAL WORLDS

Some larger brand marketers are experimenting with virtual worlds, which are computer-based simulated environments intended for its users to inhabit and interact via avatars. This habitation usually is represented in the form of two- or three-dimensional graphical representations of humanoids (or other graphical or text-based avatars). Some, but not all, virtual worlds allow for multiple users.

Leading virtual worlds include Second Life (secondlife.com), ActiveWorlds (activeworlds.com), Moove (moove.com), and There.com (there.com). Many advertisers find that these are great places to promote their products, because many people surfing the sites are influencers of product usage—especially in their peer groups.

Check out the sites mentioned here and see if they're right for you and your online boutique. You'll never know until you try.

directories. You just might find the currency converter, calendar, or search function you've been looking for—already in widget form and ready for your site.

Fundamental Steps to Take with Social Media

Now that you've received an overview of social media techniques, the following are some fundamental steps to take if you'd like to experiment in this area.

➡ *Declare who you are to the online community.* If not, nobody will know you and most people do not like associating with total strangers. A great way to do this is to create an "About Us" page and list your achievements and skills.

➡ *Create a MySpace page and link your bio in the "About Us" page to your "My Space" page.* Also provide a link back from your "My Space" page to your website.

➡ *Spend an hour every week developing your online social network in MySpace.* Invite a few of these new friends to write blog articles at your site about your products or services.

➡ *Install free blog software and start publishing at least one article in your blog.*

➡ *Write articles on your site and blog, and provide an action button for each article.* The action button takes users to the submission page of the bookmarking sites.

➡ *Provide a forum at your site for users to discuss your products and services.* Don't delete negative comments because they provide insights into the improvements needed to serve your visitors better. However, censor hateful and meaningless contents. Then, register your forum at Board Tracker (board tracker.com), a forum search engine. Allow users to review and rate your products. This will help you in inventory management because you may want to discontinue low-rated products.

> ## CLICK TIP
>
> Check out Style Hive (Stylehive.com), an online style club for people who live for fashion, design, and shopping. It's where you meet your style muses and follow them as they discover and share their latest finds. This site allows users to publish images and links of cool design and fashion. Prices and links to your online boutique are allowed.

- *Provide RSS feeds for your new products, blogs, forum postings, etc.* An RSS feed provides teasers of your contents. Users will use RSS readers to scan your teasers and visit your site for more information if the teasers draw their attentions.

- *Publish all your feeds at FeedBurner.* FeedBurner provides media distribution and audience engagement services for RSS feeds. It also provides an advertising network for your feeds. If you have quality contents, you will be able to utilize the contents using its services.

- *Create how-to or new product videos and post these videos in social video sharing sites like YouTube, and Google video.* Provide a few start and end frames in these videos to introduce your site with your site URL. Post these videos using catchy titles, teasing descriptions, and appropriate tags to make them discoverable.

- *Provide embedded links to your posted videos in your site.* This will save your bandwidth and storage space because the videos reside in the video sharing sites.

- *Besides videos, use social photo sharing sites to share pictures related to contents in your site.* Use the same title, description, and tag techniques discussed earlier for social video sites.

- *Provide a "Send to Friend" feature for all products and services you offer.* This feature is a link that sends the article, product description, etc. to a recipient via e-mail. For starters, Yahoo provides a service called Action Buttons (publisher.yahoo.com/social_media_tools) that add links to your website for users to share, save, and blog about your website. Essentially, they make the Yahoo! action buttons use del.icio.us for social bookmarking and Yahoo! blog site for blogging. It also has a print feature.

Social media marketing is here to stay and will bring in profound changes to web surfers' experiences. It is the right time for implementing features to make your site social media friendly.

Before joining any social networking sites, take a close look at before signing up. What stage is the service in? If it is in alpha, it might change considerably when (and if) it reaches its final form. How much traffic does it get?

EBAY 2.0

eBay, the behemoth of online auctions and community, made up of more than 193 million registered users worldwide, has added many Web 2.0/social networking features over the past few years. Here are a few:

➡ *eBay Wiki Community*. Here, members can quickly and easily publish, contribute to, and refine articles about tips and tricks, best practices, and other topics of interest to the greater eBay community. The eBay Wiki allows anyone, even those without programming experience, to create and edit pages. Because the articles on the eBay Wiki are user-generated and based on facts and real users' experiences, the eBay Wiki becomes a valuable reference guide as more articles are published, edited, and shared (ebaywiki.com).

➡ *eBay Member Blogs*. Here, eBay users can create and publish journal-like entries within their own dedicated space on eBay. Blogs allow users to create their own content about topics that interest them and are a great way for members to share ongoing conversations with others. eBay bloggers can share personal experiences, discuss their favorite categories, and post photos, include links to other websites, and allow visitors to post comments on their blogs. In addition, users are able to tag content with relevant keywords to help other users find their content through a search on the site. eBay blogs are RSS-enabled (blogs.ebay.com).

➡ *eBay Reviews & Guides*. With eBay Reviews, eBay members may rate and share their opinions about products such as books and DVDs. With eBay Guides, members can share their expertise on any topic or category. Guides also allow you to be creative in both the topic and design the page. You can write a simple review (for example, analyze a movie you've seen) or give first-hand information about an electronic product (perhaps you're a digital camera expert). This is your opportunity to share your opinions and expertise and to help others in the community. Writers can insert pictures, special formatting, eBay links, and headings. Like reviews, guides can be voted on by readers. The most popular guides may appear on the Reviews & Guides home page (reviews.ebay.com).

EBAY 2.0, CONTINUED

➡ *eBay My World*. This is an updated profile page that enables you to showcase your personality and interests by combining many of the features already available on eBay. You automatically get an eBay My World page when you become an eBay member. When you customize your eBay My World page, you can add features and include what makes you unique. You can add links to the items you sell, photographs of yourself, highlights from your eBay blog, and a guest book so that visitors to your page can leave comments and notes for you. Then tell everyone you know to visit you (myworld.ebay.com).

(Alexa.com can give you statistics.) Finally, what do you receive for contributing free content?

Be careful not to underestimate the true cost of free services. If you sign up for too many and spread yourself too thin, you are losing time you could devote to other aspects of your business. Look at the traffic logs provided by your website's ISP or install tracking software (StatCounter [statcounter.com] and ShinyStat [shinystat.com] offer free versions, as do many others) to find out which of these services actually refers visitors to your website.

Chapter 11

Keeping Your Site Sticky

*Y*our online boutique is up. You have visitors finding you on search engines or through other forms of advertising. Customers have signed up for your e-letter and are visiting your site regularly. But how do you keep visitors on your site, searching around, and buying more? Simple: Make it sticky.

Stick It to Me

Sticky is the dream that keeps website builders going. When your site is sticky, visitors hang around. That means they're reading and buying—and you can bet that every minute a surfer sticks to your site translates into greater brand awareness for you. The stickiest sites have good content that gives users reasons to linger, to absorb more of what you're offering, as well as a site that is easy to navigate. Here are some concrete building blocks for making any site stickier:

➡ *Good copy.* The web is all about text and words. Make sure you stick to your expertise and think snappy and useful. Also, try to provide information readers can't easily find on thousands of other websites.

➡ *Easy navigation.* Every web master has a few favorite awful sites that offer great content but that nobody will ever see because they're too hard to find. Simplicity has to be a byword for any site builder, because the price of boring or confusing a visitor is that surfer's quick exit.

➡ *Gift tools.* Naturally, the end-of-year holiday season is a boon to online boutique owners. But what about the rest of the year? The truth is, your customers purchase gifts year-round—and designing your site to appeal to gift buyers any month of the year will encourage additional sales. You can appeal to these gift buyers by making it easy for customers to purchase a gift. Add a gift suggestion section to your site (and make sure to keep it updated), offer a gift registry service, sell gift certificates and gift cards/messages, and offer gift wrap.

➡ *Rich media.* Now that most of your customers and prospects probably have broadband connections, a great way to show off the merchandise in your online boutique is to offer rich media features such as zoom, virtual e-catalogs, and dynamic color-swatching.

In addition, because you are selling high-value merchandise, understand that your customers or prospects want to know—and see—everything about the merchandise they are buying, down to the smallest, most minute details. That's why rich media is a must for online boutique owners.

Rich media requires that you make sure all your content is consistent and of the best quality, and your rich media vendor can scale to allow you to leverage your rich media across all products and pages, including the homepage, thumbnail pages, product pages, shopping cart, and so on. Maximize your rich media investment by using dynamically served imagery not only to up-sell and cross-sell additional products but also to showcase items in your customers' shopping carts, on compare pages, in search results, and more. But also make sure not to put too much whiz bang in your site or add design elements just for design's sake. Make sure there is a reason for every rich media addition you make. As we've said before, a good, clean design is most important.

Adding a Site Search Tool

In general, a website search tool gives visitors to your online boutique a chance to find products on your site by searching. It acts much like a search engine. Because your site is focused on a particular area or topic, a site search tool allows visitors to find information quickly and without wading through hundreds of irrelevant results. It keeps people on your site and allows you to learn more about what your visitors are looking for.

Sites that benefit from search tools are those with valuable data on many pages as well as sites that get many visitors arriving from search engines at pages deep within the site hierarchy, and growing sites that are adding new and valuable information.

Before adding a search box, think about where one would fit in your page design. Add meta keyword tags and descriptions to your pages; that will also improve your look and feel when your page summaries are displayed by search engines.

If you are running a hosted site, ask your ISP what search services it provides. You may have to pay additional fees for search tools. If it does not provide these tools, check with friends who have servers. A search engine does not have to reside on the local server.

For more information about site search tools, check SearchTools.com (searchtools.com), a site that provides information, news, and advice about website searching technology. It is maintained by Search Tools Consulting as a service to the web community.

STICKY CHECKLIST

If you want to sell more luxury to the customers who arrive at your website, you need to offer a selection of merchandise in styles and price ranges that people fall in love with. But in addition to that, the "usability" experience your visitors have while shopping on your website is also crucial. Remember: Because you're not there in person to guide them through the sale, your site has to do that for you. So it's important to remove any barriers your customers might have in getting around your site, finding what they want, and checking out.

Your online boutique doesn't have to have all of the following functions, but usability studies show that these features increase online sales. Adding even a few to your site can help you sell more luxury items.

Website Features

- ❏ Site map
- ❏ FAQs (frequently asked questions)
- ❏ Site-search or product-search feature
- ❏ Contact form/easily visible e-mail address
- ❏ Size chart/other help with choosing the right product size
- ❏ Clear website navigation links
- ❏ "About" page that introduces the product designer and establishes a relationship with customers
- ❏ Wish-list feature
- ❏ Refer-a-friend/tell-a-friend feature

Product Images

- ❏ Ability to zoom in/click to enlarge images
- ❏ More than one view of each product, including close-ups of details
- ❏ Images showing all the colors or other options available for a particular style

STICKY CHECKLIST, CONTINUED

On-Site Marketing

- ❏ Featured item page
- ❏ Clearance sale page
- ❏ Promotion of best-selling items
- ❏ Online-only sale
- ❏ Targeted gift ideas (stocking stuffer gift ideas, teacher gift ideas, niece gift ideas, etc.)
- ❏ Volume discounts (save money when you buy more than one of an item)
- ❏ Cross-selling (recommend and link to related products on your site)
- ❏ Testimonials/customer reviews
- ❏ Gift certificates

Checkout/Payment

- ❏ Accept credit cards
- ❏ Accept debit cards
- ❏ Accept PayPal
- ❏ Accept checks/money orders
- ❏ Redeem gift certificates
- ❏ Loyalty/repeat customer/club discount or bonus
- ❏ First-time buyer discount

Shipping/Delivery

- ❏ Option to buy online, then pick up the order from your studio
- ❏ Free standard shipping
- ❏ Free upgrade to a faster shipping method
- ❏ Holiday shipping deadlines calendar

STICKY CHECKLIST, CONTINUED

Customer Service

- ❏ Personalized e-mail or autoresponder messages (with customer's name and possibly other personal details inserted)
- ❏ Faster order fulfillment option
- ❏ Free gift wrap
- ❏ E-mail newsletter to keep customers updated on your products, news, events, and specials
- ❏ Blog to keep customers updated on your products, news, events, and specials
- ❏ Privacy statement
- ❏ Assurance of secure online payment

Basically, your website needs to give people the most user-friendly online shopping experience possible, while making them feel completely secure about buying from your site.

Your Customers Online

The next section discusses some techniques for growing your online boutique now that you are already set up and beginning to get customers. And the best way to find out what your customers are doing online is to ask them. Many online boutique owners today have great relationships with their customers, and as a result, communicate with them regularly. Why not do the same, and simply ask your customers what they want? Send e-mails out to 10 to 25 regular customers, and then read every answer that comes in. Simply put, if you want to find out ways to run your business better, look at it as customers do.

You can also use web analytics to track what your customers are doing online—and to tell you whether or not you should change your site. You can also use the tools to see what products they are buying—as well as which ones they are not.

As SaladoJewelry.com's Valentine says, "The most important thing you can do is keep your site sticky, so when people come there, they stay and buy . . . [But] you better use web analytics on your site to see what they do, and constantly change the site to keep it interesting."

What are web analytics? Basically, it is the study of the behavior of website visitors. In a commercial context, it refers to the use of data collected from a website to determine what aspects of the website work toward the business objectives. For example, it studies which landing pages encourage people to make a purchase.

Data collected almost always includes web traffic reports, but it may also include e-mail response rates, direct mail campaign data, sales and lead information, or other custom metrics as needed. This data is typically compared against key performance indicators for performance, and used to improve a website or marketing campaign's audience response.

There are many third-party software tools designed to dissect log files and automatically produce spiffy, usable reports that will tell you not only which countries are producing visitors but also their ISPs and more. The products and services today also allow you to do things like website optimization, which allows you to track how people behave on your site and then using that information, to optimize it in the best way possible.

Perhaps the best service for a startup online boutique is Google Analytics (google.com/analytics), a free web analytics service that measures the effectiveness of websites and online marketing campaigns.

Google Analytics allows customers of its AdWords service (Google's pay-per-click program where online boutique owners can create their own ads and choose keywords) to see exactly how visitors interact with their website and how their advertising campaigns are faring. Website owners can see exactly where visitors come from, which links on the site are getting the most traffic, which pages visitors are viewing, how long people stay on the site, which products on merchant sites are being sold, and where people give up in multistep checkout processes.

Marketers can also use the service to track banner, e-mail, and non-paid and paid search advertising campaigns from other ad service providers. That service is free even if companies do not advertise with AdWords, as

THE ABCS OF A/B TESTING

As your online boutique grows, you may want to try A/B testing, also known as A/B split testing, which allows you to test two different versions of your website. You can measure how customers respond to both versions and then optimize the site based on that information. Coremetrics (coremetrics.com), Omniture (omniture.com), and WebTrends (webtrends.com) are three leading companies that offer A/B testing; services run about $10,000 per month.

To be effective, A/B testing should be ongoing—your best page will change over time, so it's important to continue testing. Other tips:

➡ *Run tests on the registration or shopping cart page.* Improving these areas generally provides the greatest impact on the bottom line.

➡ *For big impact, focus on big elements.* Small changes to small elements nearly always yield small results. Instead of testing text color, font size, or font type, focus on big elements such as product, pricing, primary copy, images, offers and calls-to-action.

➡ *Test heavily-trafficked campaigns in a time frame of two weeks or less.* This creates better answers fast.

long as the users do not view more than 5 million web pages in a given month.

Tweaking and retweaking her site is all part of the process for PurePearls.com's Raab. "We are always striving to make PurePearls.com a more user-friendly online boutique that had quality products that customers must have," she says. "We add new products to our line every month and tweak the site on a weekly basis. PurePearls.com is in a constant state of testing to see what works and what doesn't in an effort to improve customer experiences."

Usability Testing

A great way to check how your online boutique is performing is using usability testing. In general, usability testing is a technique used by many online boutiques to evaluate their website by testing it on users. Rather than showing users a rough draft and asking, "Do you understand this?", usability testing involves watching people trying to use something for its intended purpose. This can be a great benefit because it gives direct input on how real users use your website.

During usability testing, online boutique owners observe people using their site in an effort to discover errors and areas that need improvement. Usability testing generally involves measuring how well test subjects respond in four areas:

1. *Efficiency.* How long does it take people to complete basic tasks? For example, find something to buy, create a new account, and order the item?
2. *Accuracy.* How many mistakes did people make? Were they fatal or recoverable with the right information?
3. *Recall.* How much does the person remember afterwards or after periods of nonuse?
4. *Emotional response.* How does the person feel about the tasks completed? Is the person confident or stressed? Would the user recommend this system to a friend?

The results of the first test can be treated as a baseline or control measurement. All subsequent tests can then be compared to the baseline to indicate improvement.

Setting up a usability test involves carefully creating a scenario, or realistic situation, wherein the person performs a list of tasks using the product being tested while observers watch and take notes. Techniques popularly used to gather data during a usability test include think-aloud protocol, where the person doing the test talks aloud about why they are doing certain things on the site and eye tracking, where the observer's eyes are tracked on the site, to see where they are looking—or not looking. There are several companies that offer eye-tracking software or services; to find one just do a Google search.

Several other test instruments such as scripted instructions, paper prototypes, and pre- and post-test questionnaires are also used to gather feedback on the website being tested. For example, to test the navigation elements of a website, a scenario would describe a situation in which a person needs to search the site to find a certain type of product, they would be asked to undertake this task.

Again, the aim is to observe how people function in a realistic manner, so that online boutique owners can see problem areas as well as what people like.

Some people think that usability is very costly and complex and that user tests should be reserved for the rare web design project with a huge budget and a lavish time schedule. This is not the case. Elaborate usability tests are a waste of resources. Studies show that the best results come from testing no more than five users and running as many small tests as you can afford.

Try usability testing. You won't believe how much you can learn by sitting silently behind someone—hopefully someone objective and not a friend or family member—and watching them browse your site. Start them off by giving the observer some generic directions, such as "You're shopping for a fun handbag."

But be careful what you wish for. It might feel great when your tester finds that they have no problem navigating your site and says they feel confident shopping on it because of your privacy and security notices. But don't get discouraged if they find glitches in things as essential as the checkout process. Remember: This information can help improve your online boutique. If the tester is having trouble with the checkout process, use the feedback to streamline it.

The website design and traffic building is a constant process of improvement. You'll feel so much better about your online boutique after seeing someone else use it.

Chapter 12

Tapping International Markets

*O*ne of the lures of the web is that once your online boutique is up, you are open for business around the world 24 hours a day. But don't be too quick to take the hype at face value. Yep, you are open 24/7, but international sales may prove elusive. And even when you land orders from abroad, you may wonder if they're worth the bother. Shocked?

There are excellent reasons for many online boutiques to aggressively pursue global business, but before you let yourself get dazzled by the upside, chew on the negatives. Then, once you have seen that foreign customers represent their own hassles but you still want them, you will find the information you need to grab plenty of international sales. After all, despite the headaches, many overseas buyers do purchase luxury items online.

Foreign Affairs

Here's the root of the problem with selling internationally: Whenever you ship abroad, you enter into a complicated maze of the other country's laws. Let's assume you're in the United States. You know Uncle Sam's laws, and you know that one neat thing about doing business in the United States is that barriers against interstate commerce are few. For a Nevada e-tailer to ship to California is no more complicated than putting the gizmo in a box and dropping it off at the post office. With some exceptions, few e-tailers collect sales tax on interstate sales. (For more on internet sales tax, see Chapter 6.)

Sell abroad, however, and it's a quick step into a maze of complexities, including customs, for instance. Generally, it's up to the buyer (not you) to pay any customs owed, but make sure your buyers know that additional charges—imposed by their home countries and payable directly to them—may be owed. You can pick up the forms you'll need at any U.S. post office.

Some countries also charge a national sales tax, or a value-added tax (around 20 percent on many items in many European countries). Again, as a small foreign retailer, you can pretty safely not worry about collecting these monies, but your buyers may (and probably will) be asked to pay, and they need to understand this is not a charge on your end.

Mailing costs, too, escalate for foreign shipments. Airmail is the best way to go for just about any package, and that gets pricey. A one-pound parcel post shipment to Europe costs more than $10, for instance. Insurance, too, is a must for most shipments abroad, mainly because the more miles a package travels, the more chance of damage or loss. Costs are low (insuring a $100 item costs about $2.50 via the U.S. Postal Service), but they still add to the charges you've got to pass on to the customer. Add up the many fees—customs,

---

CLICK TIP

It's tempting: Declare that an item is an unsolicited gift, and the recipient often doesn't have to pay any customs charges. The amount that can be exempted varies from country to country; usually it's $50 to $100. But don't make that declaration even if a buyer asks (and savvy ones frequently will)—they are asking you to break the law.

---

value-added taxes, postage, insurance—and what might initially seem a bargain price to a buyer can easily be nudged into the stratosphere.

Getting authorization on foreign credit cards can also be time-consuming. Although many major U.S. cards are well-entrenched abroad (especially American Express and Diner's Club) and validating them for a foreign cardholder is frequently not difficult, as a rule this process is fraught with risks for the merchant. Be careful.

All Aboard

If you're still not discouraged, do one more reality check to make sure international sales make sense for you. Is what you are selling readily available outside your country? Will what you sell ship reasonably easily and at a favorable price? Even with the costs of shipping factored in, will buying from you rather than from domestic sellers be a benefit to your customers? If you pass these tests, you are ready to get down to business.

Step one in getting more global business is to make your site as friendly as possible to foreign customers. Does this mean you need to offer the site in multiple languages? For very large companies, yes. American Express, for instance, has over 60 worldwide sites accessible at americanexpress.com, and many of them are written in different languages. But the costs of doing a good translation are steep. Worse, whenever you modify pages—which ought to be regularly—you'll need to get the new material translated, too.

Small sites can usually get away with using English only and still be able to prosper abroad. Consider this: When you search for homes for sale on

> ## CLICK TIP
>
> When is a foreign customer not a foreign customer? When they want you to ship to a U.S. address. Perhaps an Edinburgh father is sending a birthday gift to his daughter at a Boston college. Or when the customer is an American in the military or diplomatic corps. Shipping to their addresses is no different from mailing to a domestic address. Don't judge an e-mail address by its domain. The address may end in "it" (Italy) or "de" (Germany), but it can still be a U.S. order.

Greek islands, you'll find as many sites in English as in Greek. Why English? Because it has emerged as an international language. A merchant in Athens will probably know English because it lets him talk with French, German, Dutch, Turkish, and Italian customers. An English-only website will find fluent readers in many nations. Just keep the English on your site as simple and as traditional as possible. The latest slang may not have made its way to English-speakers in Istanbul or Tokyo.

To make your online boutique more user-friendly to foreign customers, put up a page—clearly marked—filled with tips especially for them. If you have the budget, get this one page translated into various key languages. (A local college student might do a one-page translation for around $20.) Use this space to explain the complexities involved in buying abroad. Cover many of the hassles we just discussed, but rephrase the material so that it looks at matters through the buyer's eyes. By all means, include the benefits, too, but don't leave anything out. The more clear a customer's thinking is before pressing the "Buy" button, the more likely they are to complete the transaction.

In the meantime, routinely scan your log files in a hunt for any patterns of international activity. If you notice that, say, Norway is producing a stream of visitors and no orders, that may prompt you to search for ways to coax Norwegians into buying. Try including a daily special "for Norwegian mailing addresses only" or perhaps running a poll directed at Norwegians.

Clues about foreign visitors will also help you select places to advertise your site. While an ad campaign on Yahoo! may be beyond your budget, it's entirely realistic to explore, say, ads on Yahoo! Sweden. If you notice an

OH, CANADA!

Although Canadians still lag a bit behind U.S. consumers when it comes to online shopping, that's starting to change. According to a June 2006 survey by J.C. Williams Group (jcwg.com) of 1,312 Canadians who had purchased online in the past six months, 32 percent made five or more purchases and 68 percent made one to four purchases. Canadian e-commerce is growing substantially as well, with e-commerce sales totaling $32.4 billion ($39.2 billion Cdn) in 2005, up 38.4 percent from 2004.

"U.S. retailers are looking for expansion possibilities internationally, and Canada is a friendly way to test systems and processes in an initial expansion strategy," says Maris Daugherty, senior consultant of multichannel practice at J.C. Williams Group in Chicago. "In addition, U.S. retailers are not too far from home, and there is untapped demand in Canada, and many Canadian retailers have not yet included e-commerce among their sales channels."

To design a website that meets the needs of Canadians, use a single e-commerce platform that supports all countries. "The platform should have the ability to be centrally supported with localized content areas and processes defined by country, so the customer can choose their country of preference when they arrive, and it will then be customized by specific cultural options," Daugherty says. "In Canada, that would include language options in French or English, total pricing including sales tax and shipping charges represented in Canadian Dollars, and customer service hours that reflect Canadian regions with availability to both English- and French-speaking agents."

increase in visitors (or buyers!) from a specific country, explore the cost of mounting a marketing campaign that explicitly targets them.

At the end of the day, whether you reap substantial foreign orders or not is up to you. If you want them, they can be grabbed because the promise of the web is true in the sense that it wipes out time zones, borders, and other barriers to commerce. That doesn't mean these transactions are easy—they can be

CLICK TIP

Want a no-cost translation of your site? Offer a link to PROMT-
Online, a free online translation service (translation2.paralink.com).
Before putting this up, however, ask friends—or pay an expert—to take a look at the
translation. These types of services usually offer excellent translations, but you don't
want your site's translation to be the embarrassing exception.

challenging, as you've seen—but for the e-commerce entrepreneur determined
to sell globally, there is no better tool than the web.

Online Boutique Resources

*L*isted below are online resources mentioned in the book. These resources, solutions, and tools will help you build your online boutique.

Affiliate Marketing Programs

Associate Programs, associateprograms.com
Click Booth, clickbooth.com

Commission Junction, cju.cj.com

Commission Soup, commissionsoup.com

LinkShare, linkshare.com

Blogging Software

Blogger, blogger.com

Feedburner, feedburner.com

Pingoat, pingoat.com

Slide, slide.com

TypePad, typepad.com

Wordpress, wordpress.com

Business Software

Act! (Sage Software), act.com

Microsoft Money, microsoft.com

Microsoft Office, microsoft.com

Microsoft Outlook, microsoft.com

Microsoft's Windows Vista, microsoft.com

QuickBooks, Intuit Software, quickbooks.intuit.com

Click-to-Call Providers

Art Technology Group Inc./eStara, estara.com

LiveOffice LLC, liveoffice.com

LivePerson Inc., liveperson.com

Comparison Shopping Sites

AOL Shopping, shopping.aol.com

BizRate, bizrate.com

Google Product Search, google.com/products

NexTag, nextag.com

PriceGrabber, pricegrabber.com

Shopping.com, shopping.com

Shopzilla.com, shopzilla.com

Yahoo! Shopping, shopping.yahoo.com

Domain Name Registrars

GoDaddy Group Inc., godaddy.com

Network Solutions Inc., networksolutions.com

Register.com, register.com

E-Commerce/Online Boutique Research

Census Bureau, census.gov

comScore Inc., comscore.com

eMarketer Inc., emarketer.com

The e-tailing group inc., e-tailing.com

Forrester Research, forrester.com

Interactive Advertising Bureau, iab.net

The International Diamond and Jewelry Exchange, idexonline.com

Internet Retailer magazine, internetretailer.com

J.C. Williams Group, jcwg.com

JupiterResearch LLC, jupiterresearch.com

The Luxury Institute, luxuryinstitute.com

Society for New Communications Research, SNCR, sncr.org

U.S. Department of Commerce, doc.gov

Unity Marketing, unitymarketingonline.com

E-Mail Service Providers/E-Mail Resources

Constant Contact, constantcontact.com

The Direct Marketing Association, the-dma.org

ExactTarget, exattarget.com

Federal Trade Commission, ftc.gov

Google Groups, groups.google.com

Topica, topica.com

Instant Chat Resources

Gabbly, gabbly.com

Karzi.com, karzi.com

Office Supply Resources

NexTag.com, nextag.com

Office Depot, officedepot.com

OfficeMax, officemax.com

Staples, staples.com

Online Fulfillment Resources

DHL, dhl.com

Endicia.com, endicia.com

FedEx Corp., fedex.com

iShip Inc., iship.com

Newgistics Inc., newgistics.com,

Pak Mail, pakmail.com

Red Roller Inc., redroller.com

U.S. Postal Service, usps.com

UPS Inc., ups.com

Online Payment Resources

Authorize.net, authorize.net

Bill Me Later Inc., bill-me-later.com

Google Checkout, checkout.google.com

PayPal, paypal.com

SkipJack Financial Services Inc., skipjack.com

VeriSign Inc., verisign.com

Visa's PCI DSS, usa.visa.com/merchants/risk_management/cisp.html

Online Press Release Services

24-7 Press Release, 24-7pressrelease.com

Marketwire, marketwire.com

PRBuzz.com, prbuzz.com

PRWeb, prweb.com

Online Product Reviews

Bazaarvoice, bazaarvoice.com

PowerReviews, powerreviews.com

Prospero, prospero.com

Online Sales Tax Resources

DavidHardesty.com, davidhardesty.com

The Sales Tax Institute, salestaxinstitute.com

Streamlined Sales Tax Governing Board Inc., streamlinedsalestax.org

Photography/Photo Editing Resources

Adobe, adobe.com

Adobe Stock Photos, adobe.com/products/creativesuite/stockphotos

Amvona.com Inc., amvona.com

Apple's iPhoto/Apple's Aperture, apple.com

BigStockPhoto, bigstockphoto.com

Canon USA Inc., usa.canon.com/consumer

Comstock, comstock.com

eBay Inc., ebay.com

eFashionSolutions/eFashionStudio,
    efashionsolutions.com/efasionstudio.com

FotoSearch, fotosearch.com

iStockPhoto.com, istockphoto.com

Microsoft, office.microsoft.com/en-us/clipart/default.aspx

Photography Lighting Company, photography-lighting.com

Shutterstock, shutterstock.com

Privacy Seals

BBBOnline, bbbonline.com

TRUSTe.org, truste.org

Search Engines/Search Engine Resources

Google AdWords, adwords.google.com, https://adwords.google.com/select

Google Inc., google.com

Microsoft adCenter, https://adcenter.microsoft.com, advertising.msn.com

Open Directory Project, dmoz.com

Search Engine Watch, searchenginewatch.com

WebTrend Inc.'s WebPosition, webposition.comYahoo! Inc., Yahoo.com

Yahoo! Directory, docs.yahoo.com/info/suggest/submit.html

Yahoo! Search Marketing, searchmarketing.yahoo.com,
    searchmarketing.Yahoo.com/local

Searchandising Solutions

Celebros, celebros.com

Mercado Software, mercado.com

SLI Systems, sli-systems.com

Security Seals

GeoTrust, geotrust.com

Hacker Safe, hackersafe.com

Thawte, thwate.com

VeriSign, verisign.com

Shopping Cart Solutions

1ShoppingCart.com, 1shoppingcart.com

osCommerce, oscommerce.com

Zen Cart, zencart.com

Small Business Resources

Entrepreneur magazine, entrepreneur.com

Entrepreneur Press, entrepreneurpress.com

FindLaw, findlaw.com

Incorporate.com, incorporate.com

Mycorporation.com, mycorporation.com

StartupNation LLC, startupnation.com

SCORE, score.org

U.S. Copyright Office, copyright.gov

U.S. Patent and Trademark Office, uspto.gov

U.S. Small Business Administration's website, sba.gov

Social Media Tools/Sites

ActiveWorlds, activeworlds.com

Audacity, audacity.com

Blinklist, blinklist.com

BoardTracker, boardtracker.com

Cartfly, cartfly.com

Cooqy, cooqy.com

Del.icio.us, del.icio.us/

Digg, digg.com

eBay Blogs, blogs.ebay.com

eBay My World, myworld.ebay.com

eBay Reviews, reviews.ebay.com

Facebook, facebook.com

Flickr, flickr.com

FormLogix, formlogix.com

Google Gadgets, google.com/webmasters/gadgets/

iLike, ilike.com

Moove, moove.com

MySpace, myspace.com

Propeller, propeller.com

Reddit, reddit.com

Second Life, secondlife.com

Shoestring Radio and Podcasting course, shoestringradio.com

Shopit, shopit.com

Squidoo, squidoo.com

Stumbleupon, stumbleupon.com

StyleHive, stylehive.com

There.com, there.com

Twitter, twitter.com

Widgetbox, widgetbox.com

YouTube, youtube.com

Stat Tracking Software

Alexa, alexa.com

ShinyStat, shinystat.com

StatCounter, statcounter.com

Turnkey e-Commerce Solutions

1&1 internet Inc., 1and1.com

eBay Inc., ebay.com

Flying Cart, flyingcart.com

GoDaddy Group Inc., godaddy.com

Google's Google Apps For Your Domain,
google.com/a/help/intl/en/index.html

Hostway Corp., hostway.com

iPower, ipower.com

Microsoft Corp.'s Microsoft Office Live, microsoft.com

Network Solutions, networksolutions.com

ProStores Inc., prostores.com

Verio Inc., verio.com

Web.com Inc., web.com

Yahoo! Small Business' Yahoo! Merchant Solutions,
smallbusiness.yahoo.com/ecommerce

Web Analytics

Coremetrics, coremetrics.com

Google Analytics, google.com/analytics

Omniture Inc., omniture.com

WebTrends Inc., webtrends.com

Video Resources

Apple's I-Movie, apple.com

Audacity, audacity.com

Microsoft's Windows Movie Maker, microsoft.com o

YouTube, youtube.com

Miscellaneous

Amazon.com Inc., amazon.com

Amazon Business Solutions, amazonservices.com

Anywho, anywho.com

Avalara, avalara.com/freetaxrates.com

BizTrade, biztradeshows.com

Elance Inc., elance.com

Etsy Inc., etsy.com

EventsEye, eventseye.com

goWholesale, gowholesale.com

Internet Retailer, internetretailer.com

Keynote NetMechanic, net mechanic.com

Kompass Integrated Solutions Inc., kompass-usa.com

Like.com, like.com

Network Solutions, networksolutions.com/cgi-bin/whois

Riya, riya.com

ROMT-Online, translation2.paralink.com

SearchTools.com, searchtools.com

Skweezer.com, skweezer.com

Tradeshow Week, tradeshowweek.com

Virid, virid.com

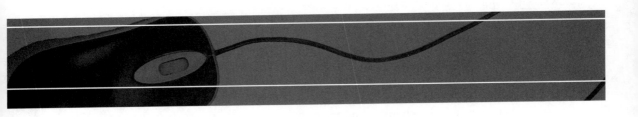

Glossary

*U*nderstanding the following terminology will help you better put all of the pieces together as you brainstorm, design, and ultimately launch your e-boutique.

Advertising. This is a paid form of communication that allows you to market and promote your products to customers by conveying your exact marketing message. As the advertiser, you have total control over the message, as well as where and when it appears or is heard. As an online business operator, advertising can be done using many forms of media, including in newspapers, magazines, radio, television, billboards and newsletters, as well as online.

Affiliate marketing. This type of marketing plan involves getting other online merchants and websites that are not direct competitors, but that appeal to your same target market, to promote your online business by displaying ads or offering links to your site on their site. In exchange, you pay that site either on a per-view or per-click basis, or offer a commission on any sales that site helps you generate through a referral.

Angel investors. These are individuals who invest in companies at an early stage in exchange for equity and the chance to help guide the company.

Blog. A shortened term for a web log, a blog is an a website maintained by an individual or company with regular entries of commentary, descriptions of events, or other content, including graphics or video.

Brick-and-mortar store. Located in the real world (as opposed to in cyberspace), a bricks-and-mortar retail store is any traditional retail establishment you'd typically find along Main Street in your neighborhood, or within a local shopping center or mall. It can be operated by a local proprietor or be part of a nationwide retail chain.

Business plan. This is a detailed written document a business operator creates when they're first brainstorming an idea for a new business venture, and they're trying to determine whether their idea is feasible. A business plan includes financial projections and forecasts, as well as a detailed description of the business' goals, strategies, operational procedures, policies, and potential.

Cable broadband service. A type of broadband internet service with an "always-on" high speed internet connection. Internet access is delivered over a cable television line utilizing "shared technology"—that is all subscribers on the system share a single connection to the internet.

Catalog page. The part of a website that showcases the specific products being sold. A catalog page can display one or more products at a time, and use text, photos, graphics, animation, audio, or other multimedia elements to help sell each product.

Content. The combination of text, graphics, photographs, animations, audio, and other multimedia elements (also called assets) used to populate and create a website.

Conversion rate. This is the percentage of people who actually make a purchase from your website, compared to the number of people who simply visit the site without making a purchase. As an online business operator, your goal is to create the highest conversion rate among your site's visitors as possible.

Cost-per-click (CPC). How much it ultimately costs for each individual web surfer to click on an online-based ad for a website in order to visit that site. Some online ads are paid for based on the number of people who view them (impressions), while others are paid for based on the number of people who actually click on the ad.

Comparison shopping sites. These sites, also known as "shopping bots," are similar to search engines except that instead of finding "information," they're designed to help shoppers find the products or services they're looking for on the internet. Shopping bot sites list specific product information so shoppers can compare features and prices.

Digital subscriber line (DSL). This type of broadband internet service provides "always-on" high speed Internet access over a single dedicated telephone line.

Distributor. An authorized representative of a product manufacturer that sells large quantities of a specific product to retailers, who them sells them in much smaller quantities to consumers. As an online business operator, you'll typically buy your inventory directly from manufacturers, distributors, importers (if the product is coming from overseas) or wholesalers.

Domain name registrar. These are the online-based services, such as Go Daddy.com and NetworkSolutions.com, where someone can register their website's domain name.

E-boutique. An e-commerce website (see below) that sells selling high-end or luxury items. These products range from clothing and leather goods to jewelry and other accessories.

E-commerce turnkey solution. A complete set of website design and management tools that allow anyone to create, publish and manage an e-commerce website for a pre-determined (often recurring) fee. These solutions require absolutely no programming knowledge. A computer with access to the Internet is required to use them, because the majority of these tools are online-based.

E-commerce website. A website designed to sell products online which will ultimately be shipped to the customer once payment is received. Thus, this type of website must quickly and accurately convey details about the product(s) being sold, plus have a shopping cart feature that allows customers (web surfers) to safely and securely place their orders using a major credit card or another online payment method.

E-mail marketing. This is a type of direct marketing that uses electronic mail as a means of communicating commercial or fundraising messages to an audience. In its broadest sense, every e-mail sent to a potential or current customer could be considered e-mail marketing.

Fulfillment. In the most general sense, fulfillment is the complete process from a point-of-sale inquiry to delivery of a product to the customer.

Google checkout. A service of Google, this is a way for e-commerce website operators to quickly and securely accept and process online payments.

Hit. A single hit is equivalent to one visitor to a website or one person viewing a specific webpage.

Homepage. This is the main page of any website. It's where a web surfer lands when they enter a website's URL into their browser software.

HTML. Stands for HyperText Markup Language. It's a popular programming language used to create web pages, online documents and websites. HTML defines the structure and layout of a webpage and allows for the use of hyperlinks.

Inventory. The amount or quantity of a specific product you have on-hand (in your warehouse, for example) to sell to your customers.

Internet Service Provider (ISP). A company or business that provides access to the internet and related services. In the past, most ISPs were run by the phone companies. In addition to internet access, they may provide a combination of services including domain name registration and hosting

Logo. A single or multi-colored graphical image that establishes a visual icon to represent a company. A logo can also make use of a specific or custom designed font or typestyle to spell out your company's name.

Mass-Market Retailer. These are large retail superstores that cater to the mass-market and carry a wide range of products. Wal-Mart and Target are examples.

Merchant. Someone who sells products or services. In terms of this book, it refers to someone selling products online using an e-commerce website.

Merchant account. Offered by a merchant account provider, such as a bank or financial institution, this is what's required for a business operator to be able to accept credit card payments. The merchant will be charged various fees to be able to accept credit cards from their customers.

Meta tag. This includes specific lines of HTML programming within your website which is used to categorize your site's content appropriately in the various search engines and web directories. In addition to the site's description, title and a list of relevant keywords, within the HTML programming of your site, you'll need to incorporate a text-based, one-line description of your site (which again utilizes keywords to describe your site's content). A meta tag must be placed within a specific area of your page's overall HTML programming.

Niche market. This is a narrowly defined group of people that make up a company's target market. The people in your niche market (or target audience) can be defined by their age, sex, income, occupation, height, weight, religion, geographic area, interests, and/or any number of other criteria.

Payment gateway. Allows a customer's credit card data to be secure as they place orders on an e-commerce website.

PayPal express checkout. A service of PayPal, this is a way for e-commerce website operators to quickly and securely accept and process online payments.

Podcast. This is simply a series of audio files that are made available for others to hear. It is called a podcast because it is usually broadcast on a regular basis like a radio show, but listeners have the convenience of listening to the podcast on their computer or MP3 player, such as an iPod. Another feature of a podcast is that its availability is often announced via RSS feed. (*See RSS Feed.*)

Product. The specific items an online business operator will be selling.

Pubic relations. A marketing strategy used to obtain free editorial coverage in the media, in the form of product reviews, interviews, and/or product mentions in news stories, for example.

Retail price. This is the price that a merchant (retailer or online business operator) sells a specific product to their customers for.

Really simple syndication (RSS) feed. These web feeds automatically deliver updated digital content—such as blog entries, news headlines, or podcasts—to subscribers

Search engine. An online service that web surfers use to find what they're looking for on the web. A search engine is a comprehensive and ever growing listing or directory of websites and their content.

Search engine marketing. Also referred to as keyword advertising. It involves paid, keyword (text-based) advertising using Yahoo! Search Engine Marketing, Google AdWords, and/or Microsoft AdCenter. This helps to drive very targeted traffic to your site easily and inexpensively. These short, text-only ads are keyword-based and appear when a potential customer enters a specific search phrase into a search engine, for example.

Search engine optimization (SEO). This involves getting your site listed with the major search engines, like Yahoo! and Google, and then working to constantly maintain and improve your ranking/positioning with each search engine so your site is easy to find and receives top placement.

Secure sockets layer (SSL) encryption. Refers to the technology used to allow for safe and secure online credit card transactions (payments) via the internet. Proper encryption helps to prevent hackers from obtaining your customers' credit card data and personal information, which could then be used to commit fraud or other crimes. SSL is used for transmitting data securely over the web.

Shopping cart. The module of an e-commerce website that serves as an interactive order form. It allows customers to input their order, shipping details, and credit card/payment information in a secure manner, and then place their order electronically through a website.

Social media marketing. This is a type of internet marketing that seeks to achieve branding and marketing communication goals through the participation in various social media networks. The central theme of these sites is user-generated content with the social aspects of allowing users to set up social communities, invite friends and share common interests.

Target audience. This is the core group of people your business' products will most appeal to and who will comprise your core customer base.

Traffic. Refers to the number of web surfers who visit your site on an hourly, daily, weekly, monthly, or annual basis. A visitor is someone who surfs over to your website to explore. Your goal as an online merchant is to transform web surfers into paying customers who ultimately place orders for your product electronically when visiting your site.

URL (uniform resource locators). This is a website address. A typical URL has three main components. The first part typically begins with "www." or "http://www." The second part of a URL is what you actually must select. The third part of a URL is its extension, which is typically ".com", however, a variety of other extensions are available, such as .edu, .org, .net, gov, .info, .TV, .biz, .name, and .us.

Venture capitalists. These are individuals or companies with large amounts of capital to invest and expect higher returns. They typically only invest in established companies.

Virtual worlds. These are computer-based simulated environments intended for its users to inhabit and interact via avatars. Many marketers uses these worlds to promote products and services.

Web analytics. This is the study of the behavior of website visitors. In a commercial context, it refers to the use of data collected from a website to determine what aspects of the website work towards the business objectives. For example, it studies which landing pages encourage people to make a purchase.

Web browser. The software used by web surfers to surf the web. Microsoft Explorer, Safari, and FireFox are examples of popular web browsers. When creating an online-based business, it's essential that your website be compatible with all of the popular browsers.

Web page. A text document that usually includes formatting and links to other pages. This special formatting is called tags, which are part of HTML and are used to link one page, section, or image to another.

Website template. Offered by e-commerce turnkey solutions, these are web page or overall web site designs that were precreated by professional designers, artists and/or programmers, and that can be fully customized to create a unique website.

Wholesale price. This is the discounted price you, the merchant, pays to purchase products in quantity from a wholesaler or distributor, for example. Once products are acquired for resale, you will then mark-up the price and sell them to your customers at each product's retail price. Part of your profit is calculated based on the difference between the wholesale price of a product, versus the price you sell the product for. All of your other business operating expenses, however, must also be taken into account.

Widgets. Also called gadgets, widgets are like mini television screens that contain information such as a brand , logo, or any interesting information pertaining to a brand that can be posted on a website, blog, or desktop. Visitors to a website with a widget on it will see it, download it, and post it on their own blogs or other sites.

Wiki. A wiki is a collection of web pages designed to enable anyone who accesses it to contribute or modify content, using a simplified markup language. Wikis are often used to create collaborative websites and to power community websites.

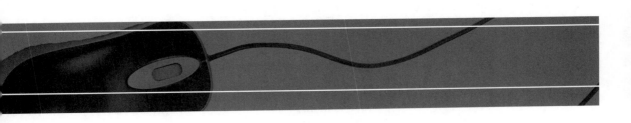

Index